Letters Home

Letters Home

The true story of Lt. Harry Frank Hunt
Veterinary Reserve Corps, American Expeditionary Forces
World War I

Compiled by Faye Converse Brown
To Commemorate the 80th Anniversary
Of the Armistice of World War I
November 11, 1918 – November 11, 1998

Daphne Publishing Company   Tucson, Arizona

Cover and illustrations by Jos Villabrille

Printed in the United States of America
Daphne Publishing Company
Tucson, Arizona

ISBN 0-9661807-0-4

First Printing: 1998

10 9 8 7 6 5 4 3 2 1

ACKNOWLEDGMENTS

The author gratefully acknowledges those who assisted in the production of this book with inspiration, information and research, photographs, creative expertise, advice and other help in bringing this project to completion.

Kevin D. Brown
Steven G. Brown
John L. Brown III
Harry Hunt Converse
Betty Converse Ennis
Virginia Converse Bohn
Penny Porter
M. Lee Knight
Karen Sheppard
Jos Villabrille
Ralph Brindle
Jack and Joyce Fulghum
Ray Brindle
Glendora Brindle
James P. Finley, Fort Huachuca Museum Historian/Director
Arizona Historical Society / Tucson Personnel
Wilson County, Kansas, Courthouse Personnel at Fredonia, Kansas
National Archives and Records Administration, Washington, DC
National Archives at College Park, MD
National Personnel Records Center, Military Personnel Records, St. Louis, MO
Kansas State University Library
Kansas State University's Sports Information Department
University of Arizona Library

Table of Contents

CHAPTER I

FAMILY TIES

Lt. Harry Frank Hunt served in the Veterinary Reserve Corps with the American Expeditionary Forces during World War I. He was my uncle, but I have only known him through the letters he wrote to his mother, Annie Sarah Hunt, and his sister, Nellie, (my grandmother and my mother) after he volunteered for Army duty in 1917.

Harry's parents, Annie Sarah Brindle and Frank M. Hunt, were married April 7, 1889, in Fredonia, Kansas, where he was superintendent of the town's water plant. She was 23 years old; he was 32. Their first child, Harry, was born November 9, 1890, and their daughter, Nellie, five years later on October 8, 1895.

Possible riches in the gold-mining business in Colorado lured Frank to accept employment at Goldfield, but before his dream could be realized, he was killed in a mine accident. Harry was but 10 years old; Nellie was five.

Annie and her children returned to Wilson County, Kansas, and lived on the John Brindle farm near Fredonia, where they were surrounded by supportive relatives. Annie had three brothers, John, William (Billy) and George, and three sisters, Nell, Flora and Jennie. John and Jennie were the only other ones who married and had children of their own, so Billy, George, Nell (also called Birdie) and Flora were especially close to Annie's fatherless two.

Many years later, one of John's sons, Ralph, said, "George was a peach of an uncle to all children; he loved children. Billy was more laid-back and reserved. Nell was an old maid, but was the only person in the world who knew exactly how a child should be raised. She was a character. Jennie had two sons, Gene and Paul Gordon. Her husband left her when they were small. Back in those days, that was a typical divorce."

Harry and Nellie attended Grand Valley School. Their transportation was by horse-drawn cart, with Nellie sitting straight and proud beside Harry as he drove the horse, Cripe. Harry loved the farm animals, especially the horses, so it was not surprising to his mother when he announced his determination to become "an animal doctor". With his goal in mind, Annie moved to Manhattan, Kansas, where Harry could enroll in the veterinary medicine curriculum at Kansas State Agricultural College.

To support her family, Annie opened a boarding house at 1010 Bluemont Street, about three blocks from the college campus. Harry gradually assumed the role of "head of the family" and protector of his mother and little sister. To Nellie he was a father figure as well as a big brother who loved to tease, occasionally giving her long, thick, dark chestnut braid a playful tug to see her dark eyes sparkle. The three were enveloped in a loving closeness that would manifest itself in his letters written them years later.

Fun-loving Harry was involved in campus activities, including being on the "famous second football team". He was initiated into the Veterinary Medical Association of the college, which had been founded in 1906, in 1910, and received his Doctor of Veterinary Medicine degree three years later.

Harry went to work with the Southwestern Serum Company in Wichita. He met a dark-haired young woman, Gesinda, called Gussie, and the two fell in love. Meanwhile, war clouds gathered over Europe. When the United States declared war on Germany in 1917, Harry registered with the draft board, but volunteered for duty before he was called. He took the examination for a commission in the Veterinary Corps at Manhattan, Kansas, on June 30, was commissioned a second lieutenant in the Veterinary Section Officers' Reserve Corps of the Army on July 20, and received the telegram ordering him to active duty on September 18. Members of the Veterinary Corps were referred to as "casuals" as they were not permanently assigned to any particular division.

*Frank and Annie Hunt
with baby Harry, born 1890*

Loomis D.A.L. Fredonia, Kans.

Nellie Hunt, born 1895

Harry, Nellie and their Father,
Frank Hunt

Nellie, Harry and
Cripe leave for school

Aunt Nell Brindle

Annie, Nellie & Harry enjoy
the funny paper

Nellie, standing, second from right

Harry and a friend

Annie & Flora Brindle

Nellie's 9th Grade Class, 1912

Nellie as a
beautiful 'teen

Nellie and chums

Nellie and school pals

Nellie

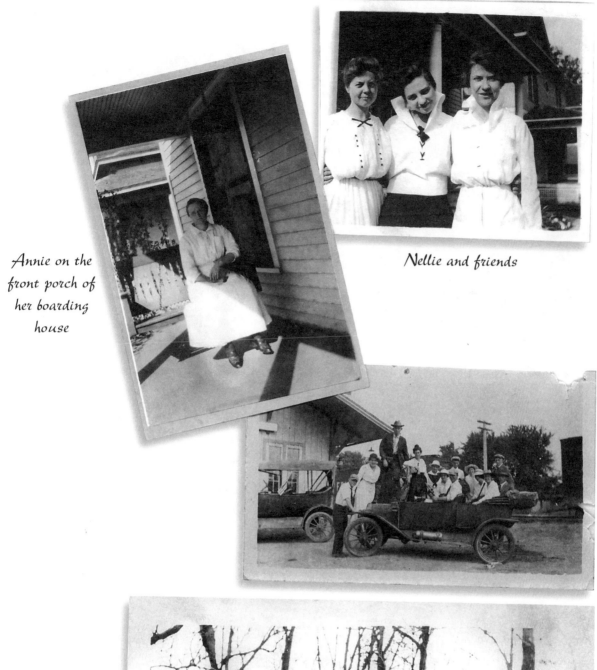

Annie on the front porch of her boarding house

Nellie and friends

Harry on an outing with college friends

Ray Olinger & Harry

Harry's graduation

Harry 1913

Ray Olinger

Nellie and friend

The Famous Second Team

Kansas Aggies~

2d Team

Annie with some of her boarders

Harry, Annie and Nellie

Kansas Aggies all in a row

Harry F. Hunt

on the KSAC Campus

Harry & Nellie

Harry loved cigars and the Elks Lodge

Nellie tries on Harry's
Army overcoat

Mrs. Annie S. Hunt

Harry & Gussie

Nellie, Annie, Harry

From "Veterinary Military History of the United States," Vol. I, by Louis A. Merillat, Lt. Col., Vet.-Res., Chief Veterinarian, First Army, American Expeditionary Forces, and Delwin M. Campbell, Lt. Col., Vet.-Res., Editor, Veterinary Medicine, Chicago, U.S.A., Veterinary Magazine Corp., 1935:

The Veterinary Reserve Corps of the Army.

"The National Defense Act of June 3, 1916, and the tentative regulations thereunder, provide for a veterinary section or branch of the officers' reserve corps. The officers of the veterinary reserve corps have the rank of second lieutenant, and are appointed and commissioned by the President, after having been found upon examination prescribed by him physically, mentally and morally qualified to hold such commissions...

"Appointees must be citizens of the United States, between 22 and 55 years of age, must be graduates of recognized veterinary colleges or universities, and must, at the time of appointment, be in the active practice of their profession in the states in which they reside."

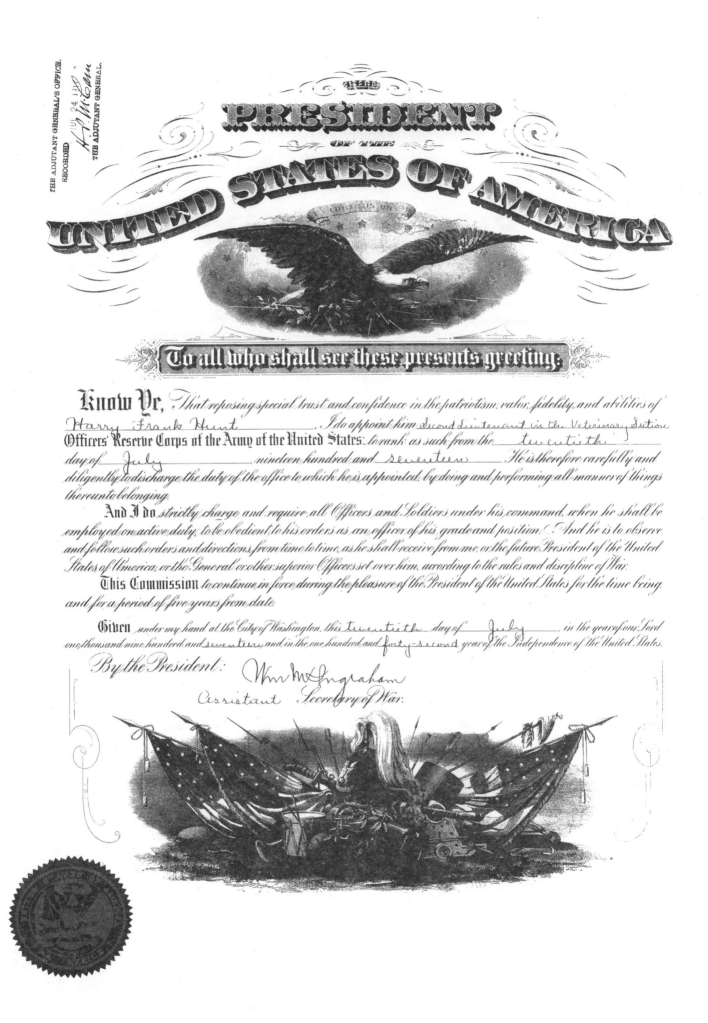

THE PRESIDENT

OF THE

UNITED STATES OF AMERICA

To all who shall see these presents greeting:

Know Ye, That reposing special trust and confidence in the patriotism, valor, fidelity, and abilities of *Harry Frank Hunt* I do appoint him *Second Lieutenant in the Veterinary Section* **Officers' Reserve Corps of the Army of the United States** to rank as such from the *twentieth* day of *July* nineteen hundred and *seventeen* He is therefore carefully and diligently to discharge the duty of the office to which he is appointed, by doing and performing all manner of things thereunto belonging.

And I do strictly charge and require all Officers and Soldiers under his command, when he shall be employed on active duty, to be obedient to his orders as an officer of his grade and position. And he is to observe and follow such orders and directions, from time to time, as he shall receive from me, or the future President of the United States of America, or the General or other superior Officers set over him, according to the rules and discipline of War.

This Commission to continue in force, during the pleasure of the President of the United States for the time being, and for a period of five years from date.

Given under my hand at the City of Washington, this *twentieth* day of *July* in the year of our Lord one thousand nine hundred and *seventeen* and in the one hundred and *forty-second* year of the Independence of the United States.

By the President:

Wm. M. Ingraham

Assistant Secretary of War.

CLASS OF SERVICE	SYMBOL
Day Message	
Day Letter	Blue
Night Message	Nite
Night Letter	N L

If none of these three symbols appears after the check (number of words) this is a day message. Otherwise its character is indicated by the symbol appearing after the check.

WESTERN UNION
TELEGRAM

NEWCOMB CARLTON, PRESIDENT   GEORGE W. E. ATKINS, FIRST VICE-PRESIDENT

CLASS OF SERVICE	SYMBOL
Day Message	
Day Letter	Blue
Night Message	Nite
Night Letter	N L

If none of these three symbols appears after the check (number of words) this is a day message. Otherwise its character is indicated by the symbol appearing after the check.

RECEIVED AT 114 AND 116 EAST FIRST ST., WICHITA, KAN.

B 445 KS V 38   GVT

DI WASHINGTON DC 3P SEP 18 1917

LIEUT HARRY F HUNT   362   234 Northern Bldg

V R C WICHITA KANS

YOU ARE ORDERED ACTIVE DUTY PROCEED TO CAMPPIKE LITTLEROCK ARK AND

REPORT IN PERSON TO COMMANDING GENERAL EIGHTY SEVENTH DIVISION FOR

DUTY TRAVEL DIRECTED NECESSARY IN MILITARY SERVICE

         MCCAIN

         310PM

Hunt
Rm
445P
Del

WAR DEPARTMENT,
WASHINGTON, *September 18, 1917.*

Extract.

*   *   *   *   *

80. Each of the following-named officers of the Veterinary Reserve Corps is ordered to active duty and will proceed to the camp indicated and report in person to the commanding general thereof for assignment to duty:

Camp Kearny, 40th Division, Linda Vista, Cal.

Second Lieut. *Charles W. Barrett.*
Second Lieut. *Fred J. Bolender.*
Second Lieut. *Curtis L. Fry.*
Second Lieut. *Sawyer A. Grover.*
Second Lieut. *Homer V. McCullah.*

Camp Upton, 77th Division, Yaphank, Long Island, N. Y.

Second Lieut. *Richard P. Head.*
Second Lieut. *John B. Lentz.*
Second Lieut. *John D. MacLeod.*
Second Lieut. *Harry M. Martin.*
Second Lieut. *William A. Steinbach.*

Camp Dix, 78th Division, Wrightstown, N. J.

Second Lieut. *Alfred T. Baeszler.*
Second Lieut. *James F. Laden.*
Second Lieut. *Theodore Schondau.*
Second Lieut. *John A. Whiting.*
Second Lieut. *Willard H. Wright.*

Camp Custer, 85th Division, Battle Creek, Mich.

Second Lieut. *Clifford J. Couchois.*
Second Lieut. *Orville E. Markley.*
Second Lieut. *Robert S. Marshall.*
Second Lieut. *Byron C. Murty.*
Second Lieut. *Reuben B. Rath.*

2

Camp Pike, 87th Division, Little Rock, Ark.

Second Lieut. *Harold J. Boyce.*
Second Lieut. *Robert H. Campbell.*
Second Lieut. *Frank W. Hueben.*
Second Lieut. *Harry F. Hunt.*

Camp Dodge, 88th Division, Des Moines, Iowa.

Second Lieut. *Russell E. Elson.*
Second Lieut. *Raymond M. Hofferd.*
Second Lieut. *Lester L. Jones.*
Second Lieut. *Lawrence A. Mosher.*
Second Lieut. *Ralph A. Moye.*
Second Lieut. *Homer S. Perdue.*

The travel directed is necessary in the military service.

*   *   *   *   *

BY ORDER OF THE SECRETARY OF WAR:

H. L. SCOTT,
Major General, Chief of Staff.

OFFICIAL:

H. P. McCAIN,
The Adjutant General.

VACCINATION REGISTER

Hunt		Harry F.	
SURNAME		CHRISTIAN NAME	

2nd Lt.		
RANK	COMPANY	REGIMENT OR STAFF CORPS

Enlisted _____, 19

At Camp Pike, Ark.

Date of birth Nov. 9, 1890 _____, 19

Triple   TYPHOID
VACCINATION AGAINST

DOSE	TEMPERATURE	DATE	INITIALS
First		9-24-17	OSM
Second	x x x x x x	Oct 1 1917	Lwm
Third	x x x x x x	oct. 8, 1917	m.g.f.

LAST PREVIOUS VACCINATION AGAINST

DATE	PLACE	NO. OF DOSES

HISTORY OF TYPHOID FEVER, IF ANY

YEAR	PLACE

PARATYPHOID
VACCINATION AGAINST

DOSE	TEMPERATURE	DATE	INITIALS
First			
Second	x x x x x x		
Third	x x x x x x		

LAST PREVIOUS VACCINATION AGAINST

DATE	PLACE	NO. OF DOSES

HISTORY OF PARATYPHOID FEVER, IF ANY

YEAR	PLACE

SMALLPOX
VACCINATION AGAINST

DATE	RESULT	INITIALS
9-24-17	Unsuccessful	OSM
10-1-17	Unsuccessful	Lwm

LAST PREVIOUS SUCCESSFUL VACCINATION AGAINST

DATE	PLACE

HISTORY OF SMALLPOX, IF ANY

YEAR	PLACE

CHAPTER II

FROM CAMP PIKE, ARKANSAS

Lt. Hunt's first letter home from Camp Pike, Arkansas, November 3, 1917.

My dear Mamma & Sister,

Your good letter received and contents noted and I will now proceed to answer it to the best of my ability. Everything going along just about as usual down here. Not very much excitement of any kind. It has been quite cool, but not cold and no snow as yet. Some of the men here from the South sure dread the cold worse than I do.

I ordered my overcoat or did I tell you. Let Nellie get her own coat and take it out of my money if you need it, because I don't want the dear girl to get cold, and then she can study harder and get out in June with the rest of the bunch. Sure wish I could get up for the K.U. game, but I want off about Xmas so will wait. Then it costs about $50.00 to make the trip to Manhattan. It is not like it was in Wichita.

Received a box of candy from a certain party in Wichita yesterday and the candy was sure good. Will have to put three cents on this letter and every one from now on, but then I suppose there will be just as many written.

I want you to send me a book out of the box, it is the largest one in there and is by (Hickra & Myrick) Therapeutics and Pathology of Dom. Animals. It is a large book with half leather black binding and the cloth is green. There are two of them and I think it is Vol. I. I want the one on infectious and contagious diseases. You can tell by looking through it because there are large articles on Tuberculosis, Rabies, Anthrax, Hemorrhagic Septicevea, Ruchipest, Hog Cholera. You might ask one of the boys about it and it is the one on contagious diseases. Send it by parcel post and be sure to insure it. Wrap it with a piece of corrugated paper first, the kind that paper boxes are made from.

Received a letter from Uncle Billy the other day and one from Billy Broberg, the latter is still in Illinois and has just been too lazy to write. Uncle Billy is still working as janitor in the hotel, but don't say anything about it, because I think Billy tells me things he doesn't tell anyone else. Of course I am not saying everything he tells me.

Sure have been enjoying the cigars. Guess you might just as well have the money in the bank, if you get a chance to lend it out on good security for a year I will give you the interest. You might try some of your relation, but you need not say I said so. I have $204.00 more I will send you soon for safekeeping.

How do you enjoy the snow, any better than other years? The sweater will be welcomed, but don't work too hard on it, because you might get sick. I am glad Nellie enjoyed her dining room work so well. Wonder if she won't take an extra session of it. From the way it looks, that is what she should specialize in. She must not make that dear man of hers (?) sick.

Believe I will quit batching when this war is over providing I can find someone to have me, and I know a certain party who is waiting patiently, somewhere in America.

I am going to town tomorrow and see the sights for a change so will ring off this time. Write soon.

Lovingly, Harry

Hdqrs. #312th Ammunition Train.
Camp Pike, Ark., Dec. 13th, 1917.

From: 2nd. Lieut. Harry F. Hunt V. R. C.

To: The Commanding General, 87th Div. Camp Pike, Ark.
           (Thru Military Channels.)

Subject: Leave of Absence.

    1.   I would request leave of absence for ten days to
become effective on or about December 22nd, 1917.

    2.   I have had no leave of absence since my appointment
as Second Lieutenant, September 22nd., 1917.

    3.   I am assigned to the 312th Ammunition Train for
Veterinary Service, there is one 2nd. Lieut. in the Veterinary
Service assigned to said Train and on duty with said Train other than
myself.

    4.   At the time I was ordered to active duty I was residing
at Wichita, Kansas., engaged in the practice of veterinary
medicine. Owing to the short time I had to report for duty after
I was called it was impossible for me to attend to my private
business affairs. I have had no opportunity to attend to said
affairs since called. If granted the leave of absence requested
I can finish my private business affairs at Wichita, Kansas and
also visit my family at Manhatten, Kansas at the same time.

                              Harry F. Hunt.

EXTRACTS FROM

GENERAL ORDERS AND BULLETINS

WAR DEPARTMENT

SEPTEMBER, 1917

RELATING TO

REGIMENTAL AND COMPANY
ADMINISTRATION

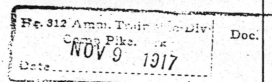

WASHINGTON
GOVERNMENT PRINTING OFFICE
1917

Camp Pike, Ark.
Feb. 11, 1918
Dear Mother and Sister:

Monday night and I am going to answer your good letter. Intended to write last night but some friends came in and it was too late when they went home for me to write. I have certainly been kept busy lately or rather I am not at the barrack very much.

I have been taking some long horseback rides here lately and certainly enjoy them and intend to continue them. Was out yesterday p.m. and rode about twenty miles way back into the hills, and Mother, I now can understand why they write so many funny stories about Arkansas.

I was out to the remount station awhile this p.m. on a little business. The weather has been almost ideal spring weather here the past week for which we are very thankful, and you know that is the kind of weather that makes a man get out and move about, especially after he has been housed up all winter on account of the cold weather.

My cold is a whole lot better and I think I will be about well in another week. Gussie sent me a dandy helmet the other day and she certainly did a good job knitting it for her first trial. The workmanship is almost perfect. Do you and she still write, or did you quit? I know she said in one of her letters not long ago that she intended to write to you soon, but I guess the dear girl has been pretty busy.

Uncle Billy is sure hot-headed about certain things but he is just too old to understand things as he should. Ex-president Taft was here Fri. and Sat. and talked and I went Fri. and he certainly gave a good talk on the war, etc.... First time I ever saw Mr. Taft and I think more of him now than I did.

That was sad about Mr. Wood. Did the children return from the coast for the funeral? I am sorry that my little sister has been sick, but she must not think of getting sick now.

I am sending you a picture of the west half of this camp but the picture was taken last fall before all of the buildings were complete. As it is past my bedtime will close so good night. Write soon.

Lovingly, Harry

Camp Pike, Ark.
Feb . 18, 1918
Dear Mamma and Nellie,

Your good letter came to hand Saturday evening and I will now proceed to answer it to the best of my ability. Everything is going just as good as could be expected down here. We have been having fine weather. The last couple of days have been pretty cool but it warmed up this evening and acts like it might rain, but I hope not. There is plenty of moisture in the ground to last for some time.

I was in town Saturday afternoon and evening and again last night. Went in Saturday to do a little shopping and attended a show and last night we went in to attend a band concert.

I have been going horseback riding about every day and certainly enjoy it. I am teaching my horse to jump some and will try to have some pictures for you soon.

I want to tell you about this income tax and how I am doing it. A head of a family is entitled to two thousand dollars and by being head of our family, which I am, in just accordance with the law, I will not have to pay any income tax so I am putting in my tax receipt as such, so govern yourselves accordingly. If there is anything you do not understand just let me know.

The boots that I spoke of in a letter some time ago were those high-top lace leather boots I bought there in Manhattan and I am going to have to have them half-soled again soon, but they are just the thing for muddy weather.

In regards to that insurance policy, I don't think that it will come for a month or so because you know they are so very busy with everything right now and it takes time but I took out the insurance just the same. I am sorry to hear that your full crew of boarders is not present but don't let anything like that worry you.

I received a very good and long letter from Ray O. the other day. He is at Camp Travis, Texas, Co. I, 90th Div. Training Camp and everything is going just fine with him. He said he intended to enlist, but before he could close out his business on the farm it was too late, so just waited for the draft and went with the first bunch, but is now attending the officers' training camp with the hopes of getting a commission. You know he was farming near Bartlesville, Okla.

Gussie is fine I guess. I received a box of fine homemade candy from her today, the best I've tasted, Mamma, but you know when you get things from certain people you like real well you naturally think more of it, but this is fine candy and there is no fooling about it.

Does Mrs. Shubert ever say anything about the war? Guess she has learned enough to keep quiet. I hope my little sister is feeling better by now. I know how it is to have a cold. Will the dear girl finish and get to graduate in June with her class?

As this is all I can think of now will ring off as I must write Gussie a letter tonight and thank her for the candy. So will bid you good night and write soon.

Lovingly, Harry

CHAPTER III

"SEND ME AWAY WITH A SMILE"

Camp Pike, Ark.
March 3, 1918
Dear Mamma & Nellie,

I am leaving here Tuesday morning for Hoboken, N.J., just received the news today. There will be five Vets in this bunch that I go with. Don't know where we are going but have kinda got an idea that I will soon be in sunny France, however, I don't know. Was somewhat surprised when I received the news but I am getting used to surprises nowadays.

It has been trying to rain here all day and finally succeeded tonight so guess we will have some mud to wade tomorrow. Will tell you about my business. My insurance policies are due in April or May, and I believe you had best pay them. I am clear in all my debts and the only money I have coming to me is the $200.00 I lent Frank Pedroja who lives in Lincoln, Kans. I am going to write him and ask him to send you a note for it, he is a good friend of mine and is good for the money, so don't worry.

I think I have enough money to carry me through so use that in the bank of mine if you need it, and if I need any I will draw on it. If at any time in the future you need help let me know and I will fix it all right. Don't let anything worry you, Mother, and remember the song that I like so well, "Send Me Away With A Smile."

Think I will wire you and Gussie tomorrow and Gussie said she intended to answer your letter soon. Remember, Mamma, that Gussie is a pretty busy girl and that is the reason she did not write. And Mamma, remember that Gussie is my little girl, to be, so take good care of her if you ever see her, and that she likes you and Nellie fine.

This is all for tonight. I am in a hurry and I am somewhat tired as I have been

packing up today. Will send a box of junk, books, etc., home and my gold watch will
be in it so better open it up and take the watch and fob out. So good night and I will
write you when I am on the train. Write me a letter and address it thus: Lieut. Harry
F. Hunt VRC, Point of Embarkation, Hoboken, N.J. Write soon as you can.
    Lovingly, Harry

Lt. Hunt started to keep a diary, but apparently gave it up in favor of writing letters shortly
after he arrived in France.

Diary entries:

Sunday, March 3, 1918:
    Received verbal orders at Camp Pike, Ark., to proceed to Hoboken.

March 4:
    Left Little Rock, Ark., for N.Y.

March 6:
    Arrived in N.Y., Martinique Hotel.

March 7:
    Reported Hoboken.

March 8:
    Received sailing orders.

March 9:
    Sailing orders delayed one day.

HEADQUARTERS 87TH DIVISION NATIONAL ARMY.

Camp Pike, Ark., March 3, 1918.

Special Orders:
  No. 62,

        1. In compliance with War Department
telegram dated March 2, 1918, the following named officers
will proceed to Hoboken, N. J., equipped for prolonged
field service, and report upon arrival to the commanding general
thereof for duty.

                1st Lieut. Harold F. Schrreck, V.R.C.N.A.
                1st Lieut. Nelson E. Southard, V. R. C. N.A.
                2nd Lieut. Oscar I. Holloway, V. R. C., N.A.
                2nd Lieut. Harry F. Hunt, V. R. C. N. A.

        The travel directed is necessary in the Military Service.

        By command of Brigadier General Van Vliet:

                                F. B. SHAW,

                            Colonel, Infantry, N.A.
                            Acting Chief of Staff.

OFFICIAL:

    W. H. DUKES,

        Adjutant General,
          Acting Adjutant.

clj.

Hdqrs. 312th Ammunition Train, 87th Div. N.A.
Camp Pike, Ark., March 4th, 1918.

From: 2nd Lieut. Harry F. Hunt

To: Adjutant General of the Army, Washington, D. C.

Subject: Departure.

1. In compliance with S.O. 62, Par. 1, Hdqrs. 87th Division National Army, Camp Pike, Arkansas dated March 3rd, 1918. Report my departure from this station March 5th, 1918 enroute to Hoboken, N. J.

Harry F. Hunt

Hdqrs. 312th Ammunition Train, 87th Div. N.A.
Camp Pike, Ark., March 4th, 1918.

From: 2nd Lieut. Harry F. Hunt, V.R.C.

To: Commanding Officer, 312th Am.Tn.

Subject: Departure.

    1.   Report my departure from this station, March 5th, 1918
enroute to Hoboken, N. J. per S.O. 62, Par.1, Hdqrs. 87th
Division, N. A. Camp Pike, Ark., dated March 3rd, 1918.

                                    Harry F. Hunt

Hoboken, N.J.
March 7,'18.

From: 2nd Lieut. Harry F. Hunt, V. R. C.

To: The Director of Vetrinary Corps, Washington, D. C.

Subject: Report of arrival.

1.   In compliance with S. O. 62, Par. 1, Headquarters
87th Division, National Army, Camp Pike, Arkansas, report
my arrival Hoboken, N. J. March 7, 1918.

                    Harry F. Hunt.

Somewhere in America,
3/5/18 (on the train)
Dear Mamma and Nellie,

I suppose you have my wire that I sent you yesterday and you should have my letter soon. I imagine you were just a little surprised to hear I was on the way. I left Little Rock last night and came via St. Louis and changed cars there. I am now on the Pennsylvania Line somewhere just west of Indianapolis. We are due to arrive in N.Y. tomorrow about 2 p.m. and don't hardly think I will report in Hoboken until the next morning. Don't know any more than I did. We may stick around the East for a month or two, and again we may go right across. If I have time, am planning on taking in some of the sights in N.Y. but that will be decided later you know.

This is pretty good country through here and everything looks fine. This is one of the warmest days in a long time and it is sure hot and dusty on this train but it's one of the best and fastest trains in this part of the country, and we are going some.

I am sending you the express receipt for the box of junk I sent you, but you should have the box before you get this letter. I told the bank in Little Rock to send a statement to you as I did not keep very close tab on my last checks.

As it is hot and I am tired will close. Write soon.

Lovingly, Harry

This letter was written March 8, 1918, on Grand Hotel, Broadway and 31st Street, letterhead:

Dear Mamma & Nellie,

I imagine you are kinda wondering where your boy is tonight, well Mamma, I am in Little Old New York and have been here for a couple of days but have been pretty busy all the time. I suppose you have the letter I sent while enroute, or you should.

Mamma, this is sure some city is all I can say and to compare it with Kansas City would be like comparing K.C. with Manhattan and believe me now, it is some town. There are street cars above you, street cars below you and street cars on a level with you. The elevated lines, the subways, and the ordinary street cars and everybody is in a hurry it seems, but such is the life of the city.

In going over to Hoboken from here we went over on the subway, that is the tunnel under the Hudson. Coming back we rode the ferry. I would say it is almost a half a mile across the river where we crossed it. Mamma, I enjoy being in this old town but don't believe I would care to live here, but it is a place to come just to see things. We went to the Hippodrome last night and a musical comedy and there were about three hundred in the chorus. Believe me, it was some show.

Was downtown today and yesterday awhile doing a little shopping and one thing I can say about N.Y., they treat you right. I bought a new serge suit better than the one I have for $29.50 and the one I have cost $40.00. Bought a pair of hightop shoes for eight and they would have cost me twenty in Little Rock and other things about the same.

Was down on Wall Street, passed the Woolworth Bldg. 59 stories high, or in other words I was just down in the heart of the big business center of N.Y. where all the large buildings are. Will write you more about it later.

We received our orders today in regards to when and where we will sail from but you know it is against orders to say anything about them. However we will be in N.Y. a few more days but how many I cannot tell you. In a short time though it will be Good-bye Broadway, Hello France.

Received your letter today forwarded from Camp Pike, also the cookies which were enjoyed very much. I am sending that Express receipt this time as I forgot it before. Will close for tonight and write more later cause I am tired and sleepy so good night. Write soon.

Lovingly, Harry
This will perhaps be my next address:
Lieut. Harry F. Hunt
c/o A.E.F.
Somewhere in France

MANGER POPULAR HOTELS

GRAND HOTEL
BROADWAY & 31ST STREET

RATES FOR GRAND HOTEL
ROOMS $1.00 & UP WITH BATH $1.50 & UP

GREAT NORTHERN HOTEL
118 WEST 57TH ST.,
NEW YORK.

HOTEL ENDICOTT
COLUMBUS AVE. & 81ST ST.,
NEW YORK.

NAVARRE HOTEL
SEVENTH AVE. & 38TH ST.,
NEW YORK.

CONTINENTAL HOTEL
9TH & CHESTNUT STS.,
PHILADELPHIA.

BELL APARTMENT HOTEL
1176 FOX STREET,
NEW YORK.

PLAZA HOTEL
NORTH AVE. & NORTH CLARK ST.,
CHICAGO.

New York 3/8/18

Dear Mamma & Nellie, and
I imagine you are kinder wondering
where your boy is tonight, Well
Mamma I am in Little Old New
York and have been here a couple
of day but have been pretty busy all
the time I suppose you have this letter
I sent while enroute or you should.
Mamma this is sure some city is
all I can say and to compare it with
Kansas City would be like comparing
K. C. with Manhattan and believe
me now it's some town, There are
street car above you street cars below you

and street cars on a level with you
The elevated lines, the subways, and
the ordinary street cars. and every
body is in a hurry it seems, but
such is the life of the city you know,
I'm going over to Hoboken from here
we went over on the subway, that's
the tunnel under the Hudson and coming
back we rode the ferry and I would say
it is almost a half a mile accross the
river when we crossed it. Mamma I
enjoy being in this old town but don't
believe I would care to live here, but
it's a place to come just to see things.
we went to the Hippodrome last night
a a musical comedy and there was
about three hundred in the chorus
and believe me it was some show,
Was down town today and yesterday a
while doing a little shopping and one
thing I can say about N.Y. they treat
you right, bought a new suit suit

MANGER POPULAR HOTELS

GRAND HOTEL
BROADWAY & 31ST STREET

RATES FOR GRAND HOTEL
ROOMS $1.00 & UP WITH BATH $1.50 & UP

GREAT NORTHERN HOTEL
118 WEST 57TH ST.,
NEW YORK.

CONTINENTAL HOTEL
9TH & CHESTNUT STS.,
PHILADELPHIA.

HOTEL ENDICOTT
COLUMBUS AVE. & 81ST ST.,
NEW YORK.

BELL APARTMENT HOTEL
1176 FOX STREET,
NEW YORK.

NAVARRE HOTEL
SEVENTH AVE. & 38TH ST.,
NEW YORK.

PLAZA HOTEL
NORTH AVE. & NORTH CLARK ST.,
CHICAGO,

New York

2

better than the one I have for $29.50 and
the one I got cost 40.00 bought a pair
of hightop shoes for eight and they
would have cost me twenty in Little Rock
and other things are about the same,
Was down on Wall St, passed the
Woolworth Bldg. 59 stories high, or in
other words I was just down in
the heart of the big business center of
N.Y. where all the large but
buildings are, Will write you more
about it later, We received our
orders today in regards to when
and where we will sail from but

you know it's against orders to
say any thing about them, However
we will be in N.Y. a few more days
but how many I cannot tell you,
In a short time though it will be
Good bye Broadway hello France
Received your letter today forwarded
from Camp P also the cookies which
were enjoyed very much. Am sending
that Express receipt this time as I
forgot it before, Will close for
tonight and write more later cause
I am tired and sleepy so good night
write soon Lovingly Harry,

This will perhaps be my next address
Lieut Harry F. Hunt
"   Co A, E, F
              Some where in
                    France

[G. O. 5.]

HEADQUARTERS PORT OF EMBARKATION,

GENERAL ORDERS, No. 5. | HOBOKEN, NEW JERSEY. January, 3, 1918.

Casual officers embarking on commercial steamers and transports will observe the following:

1. They will check their baggage immediately after assignment to stateroom, and before boarding.

2. All business must be attended to before boarding the steamer.

3. After arrival at the pier no telegrams, letters or telephone messages will be permitted to be sent from the pier, and no officer will be allowed to leave the pier except on urgent official business authorized by Commanding General, Port of Embarkation.

Furthermore, no officers will be permitted to leave the steamer after boarding except on urgent official business.

4. Boxes and bags will be placed near the gangways on ships for the reception of mail. Mail should not be sealed, but left open. Such mail is censored and forwarded as soon as practicable. No stamps necessary.

5. Arrangements should be made to have all farewells completed before arrival at the piers. No members of families, relatives or friends of those sailing will be allowed at the piers or thereabouts on day of sailing, and they must not be brought there by anyone Should any be found there they will be ordered away summarily by the guard and report made of the officer with whom they attempt to communicate.

6. Officers of the Medical and Ordnance Corps will report to representatives of their respective corps before leaving this port.

Surgeon's Office . . 209 River Street, Hoboken, N. J.
Ordnance Office . . 68 Hudson Street, Hoboken, N. J.

7. All officers will inquire for mail at the office of the Mail Censor, 310 River Street, Hoboken, N. J.

BY COMMAND OF MAJOR GENERAL SHANKS:

R. E. LONGAN,
Lieut. Col., A. G.,
Acting Chief of Staff.

OFFICIAL:

D. A. WATT,
Major, A. G. R. C.,
Adjutant.

VESSEL NO. 85

FILE NO. 39

WAR DEPARTMENT
OFFICE OF THE GENERAL SUPERINTENDENT, U.S. ARMY TRANSPORT SERVICE
TRANSPORTATION DIVISION, PASSENGER BRANCH
ROOM 412, 95 RIVER STREET, HOBOKEN, N.J.

MAR 8 - 1918

1.   Having reported at this office, this date, for transportation abroad, in compliance with order from Headquarters, Port of Embarkation, Hoboken, N.J., you will report at officers' gangway, vessel number 85
10 A.M. MAR 13 1918   North
U.S. ARMY PIER NO. 2 South Side, at Port of Embarkation, Hoboken, N.J., ready to go aboard vessel.

2.   Baggage must be at Baggage Room, U.S. Army Pier #2, Port of Embarkation, Hoboken, N.J., not earlier than two days before you report at officers' gangway, or you may bring same with you when reporting.

3.   Assignment to stateroom is given at officers' gangway. Before reporting there, claim your baggage at Baggage Room, U. S. Army Pier #2, Port of Embarkation, Hoboken, N.J., to insure it being placed aboard. When claiming baggage, mark vessel number plainly on each piece. Also mark for stateroom, or hold of ship.

4.   In the event it is necessary to communicate with this office, refer to numbers shown in the upper right-hand corner of this order.

A. C. DALTON,
Colonel, QMC.,G.S.,U.S.A.T.S.

By J. F. COGGSWELL,
Captain, Q.M.R.C.

March 7th, 1918.

CONFIDENTIAL

SPECIAL ORDERS
NO.   61.

*   *   *   *   *

3.   Upon reporting at these Headquarters in compliance with Paragraph 20 - Confidential Order No. 51 - War Department - dated March 2nd, 1918 - the following named officers will report to the Quartermaster, Port of Embarkation for assignment to first available transportation to France and upon arrival there, will report to the Commanding General, American Expeditionary Forces for duty:

Alexander, Samuel A 2d Lieut V.R.C.	Brown, William J 1st Lt V.C.NA
Conklin, Raymond LeR 1st Lt. VCNA	Courtright, John M Capt VCNA
Cox, Clifford 2nd Lieut V.R.C.	Evans, Joseph H 2d Lieut VRC
Fitzgerald, Gerald W 1st Lt VCNA	Holloway, Oscar I 2nd Lt VRC
Horcher, Charles H 2nd Lt V.R.C.	Hughes, Arthur C 2d Lt V.R.C.
Hunt, Harry F 2nd Lieut V. R. C.	Ingram, Thaddeus H Jr 2d Lt VRC
Jenkins, Lester E 2d Lieut VRC.	Jervis, Horace B.F. 2d Lt VRC.
King, Joseph E 1st Lt V.C.N.A.	Law, Buell S 2d Lieut V.R.C.
Leibold, Armin A 1st Lieut. V.C.N.A.	Lewis, Lawrence J 2d Lt V.R.C.
Lilly, Stuart C 2d Lt. V.R.C.	Lusk, William V Major V.C.N.A.
McConn, Frank J 2d Lt V.R.C.	McKim, Harry C 1st Lt V.C.N.A.
Menefee, Robert G 2d Lieut V.R.C.	Meredith, Arthur F 2d Lt VRC
Miller, Thomas I 2d Lieut V.R.C.	Morris, Harry B 2d Lt V.R.C.
Murty, Byron C 2d Lieut V.R.C.	Nickel, William C 1st Lt V.CNA
Pock, E. L., 2nd Lieut. V. R. C.	Perdue, Homer S 2d Lieut VRC
Peterson, Archa E 2d Lt V.R.C.	Reaugh, George T 1st Lt VCNA
Reinhardt, Wade H 1st Lieut VCNA	Schrear, Arthur F 2d Lt V.R.C.
Schreck, Harold F 1st Lt V.C.N.A.	Seekamp, Frederick W 2d Lt VRC
Sharp, Floyd S 2d Lt VRC	Shindelman, Samuel H 2d Lt VRC
Southard, Nelson E 2d Lt V. R. C.	Stearns, Harold E 2d Lt V.R.C.
Temple, Edwin 2d Lt V. R. C.	Weaver, Herschel J 2d Lt V.RC
Wileden, Lewis A 2d Lt V.R.C.	Worch, Francis E 1st Lt VCNA
Wright, Willard H 2d Lt V.R.C.	

The travel directed is necessary in the military service.

*   *   *   *

By command of Major General Shanks.

R. E. LONGAN,

Lieut. Colonel, A. G.,
Acting Chief of Staff.

OFFICIAL:

C. H. Dayhuff,
Major, A. G. R. C.,
Assistant Adjutant.

This document is not a passport but is issued with the approval of the Department of State.

UNITED STATES OF AMERICA.
WAR DEPARTMENT.

Form No. 633-1—A. G. O.
Ed. Dec. 26-17—5,000.

CERTIFICATE OF IDENTITY

No. _8843_

PORT OF EMBARKATION

Place ------ HOBOKEN, N. J.

Date ____ MAR 7 - 1918 ____, 191

I CERTIFY that ____ *Harry F. Hunt* ____ is an Officer of the Army of the United
(Name.)

States on detached service as *2nd Lieut Vet R.C. N.A.*
(Describe function.)

with *Casuals* and is entitled under the laws of war, if captured, to the
(Organization.)

privileges of a prisoner of war. Identification data:

27
(Age.)

brown
(Color of eyes.)

brown
(Color of hair.)

6'
(Height approximate.)

180 lbs
(Weight, approximate.)

White
(Race.)

REMARKS : *None*
(Include here notation of scars, etc., visible when clothed, which will aid in identification.)

C. H. Dayhuff.
(Signature of issuing officer.)

MAJOR, A. G.
Identification Officer
(Rank and title.)

Index finger right hand.

Tip of finger this end.

Finger print.

Harry F Hunt
(Signature of bearer.)

New York 3/12/18

My dear Mamma & Sister,

Tuesday night and I am still in Little Old New York. Think I have all my purchases made and among them bought a 2 1/2 by 4 1/4 folding Eastman Kodak and intend to have some pictures of this trip because this going to be the biggest and best trip I have ever made.

It has been pretty cold here ever since we came and has snowed a couple of times but I imagine it is always cool here this time of year. I am still wearing my B.V.D. but have some woolen ones bought and no doubt will wear them while on the boat.

Went to the Globe Theatre last night and saw the musical comedy entitled Jack O Lantern. It was very good but I did not enjoy it as much as I did the Hippodrome. Believe me things sure move in this old town and what I mean they move in a hurry.

This hotel is just a short distance from the theatre section of the city and we are only a couple of blocks from 5th Ave. which I believe is the busiest street in town. Broadway, which we are on, is also very busy and I have traveled it from 48th street to the bay. Most of the big business buildings are located down nearer the bay. You see, this part of N.Y. is just a peninsula with the Hudson and North River on one side and the East River on the other, but will tell you more about it when I see you next time. We can hear the steamers and ferry whistles plain here and you know they have a different kind of a whistle so they are easily told.

Met a couple of officers here that I knew in Kansas and they are going over soon. I guess from what the papers say a good many are moving these days. If I can I will cable you when I arrive and I want you to call up Gesina and tell her. You know her address 434 West 14th St. as I think that would be better than sending the two messages. Will also want you to phone her if someone else would notify you anything by wire concerning me.

I have one of my trunks packed and the other one almost and I am just going to see N.Y. for the rest of the time I am here which I can assure you won't be very long.

...You see a good many lady street car conductors here and I have seen several girls dressed in overalls around depots here in the East... You don't think Gussie is half as dear as I do. I think she is the dearest little girl there is and just as soon as I come back we are coming to see you again.

This is your birthday, Mamma, but I have no present for you but I am sending you my best wishes. Oh, yes, did you ever finish that sweater? As soon as I give you my address on the other side I wish you would send it. It may come in handy over there, but you know I don't believe it is as cold over there as some make out it is.

I see by the paper that the next draft is going to be called in very soon, and I am just glad of this, Mother, that I enlisted of my own free will and accord.

...Tell Nellie I know how to sympathize with her. I was once a poor wee senior, but

I will say that after you are out is when the real trouble begins. Mamma, this is all I think of now so will close for tonight. Good night and write soon.

Lovingly, Harry

My next address will be Lieut. Harry F. Hunt
V.R.C. American Expeditionary Forces
Unassigned
and that is all that is necessary to put on the envelope.

Someplace in America
Sometime in March
Dear Mother and Sister,

Just decided awhile ago that I would leave a telegram here which would be sent to you as soon as this boat arrives in France. I am leaving one here for you and Gussie, so it will not be necessary for you to phone her. This is a pretty big boat we are on and is all steel or it looks to be. Must close and mail this before we leave. Very damp, cold and foggy today.

Harry.

Diary entries:

March 13:

Spent 3/9 until today in N.Y. seeing sights.

March 14:

Reported in Hoboken Pier No. 2 and boarded transport Matsonia at 9:45 a.m. Laid in port loading until 6 p.m. when all were ordered below deck and we sailed out of port. We were not allowed on deck until about 8 p.m. Sea smooth but raining and rained most of p.m. Day very foggy and cold. Feeling fine.

March 15:

At sea. Four vessels in bunch besides guard. Transports were Pocohontas, Mallard, Alois and Matsonia. Cruiser Rochester acting as guard and several torpedo boats could be seen in the distance. Vessels were in single file early but came up abreast about 9 a.m. Beautiful sea with some whitecaps. Morning clear but chilly. Ordered out at 10:30 for lifeboat drill and order to keep our life belts on all the time.

About noon we sighted another transport, making five transports and one cruiser. The sea got rougher during the afternoon. Breakers were coming on deck. During the night the boat rocked badly. Chairs fell over in room and trunk was sliding around. Retired early and slept fine.

March 16:

At sea. Waves rolling very high, 25 to 30 feet. Cloudy and foggy with some snow. Still feeling fine. The transport we picked up I learned was the Henderson. During the night we lost transports Mallory and Alois. These 2 vessels were camouflaged. Sea was rougher and water was getting a deeper blue color. The weather was still cold. Feeling fine. Retired about 11 p.m.

March 17:

Sunday morning. Fine morning. Floating clouds but warmer due to the Gulf Stream. Picked up the two transports we lost the night before. Day very much calm and perfect. Good part of day on top deck in deck chair; also part of night.

March 18:

Raining this morning but at noon it is clearing off. Watched some of the boats have target practice. Commenced to rain again during p.m. and kept it up most of the night. Everything very foggy and stormy. Lights were shining from the top masts of all the ships. Getting colder due to leaving the Gulf Stream. Waves again were breaking over the deck and were 30 feet in height.

March 19:

Raining this morning and cold, just a slow drizzling rain. Seagulls still follow the boat. Rain most of the day. I stayed in my room reading "Mr. Grex of Monte Carlo". Stopped raining in the evening and I stayed up on deck until about 9 when I went to bed. Sea rough and rolling.

March 20:

Raining and snowing when I got up this a.m. and very cold. Northeast wind. Waves breaking over port side of deck of vessel. Spent last night on main deck from midnight. Whitecaps breaking higher and boat rolling good this a.m. Rained about all day and very disagreeable. I stayed in my room reading "The Lady of the Blue Moter". Cleared off some as night blew in.

March 21:

Raining and cloudy this a.m. Sea fairly smooth; quit raining about noon and cleared away. We passed a small tramp steamer this morning going west. Chilly up on deck this day so I stayed in my room. Had a movie show starring Bill Hart last night in the mess hall given by Y.M.C.A. Life boats were hung over side of boat today; night partially clear.

March 22:

Saw sailing vessel this a.m. early and cruiser made chase and identified it. Morning clear. Whale boat left our vessel for one of the other transports and returned with diphtheria antitoxin. At noon orders were given that no one undress until we reach port. During afternoon quite a gale came up and was blowing the waves up on top deck. Have seen no gulls following the last two days. Very disagreeable day. All must get up at 4:30 a.m. and watch.

March 23:

Sat. a.m. Cloudy and spray still coming on deck. Raining part of day. I have noticed no seagulls the last three days.

March 24:

Sunday. The day broke bright and fair with a still and quiet sea. About 9 we noticed our escort coming on the port side just at the horizon. In a very short time they were with us. They are torpedo boats and are darting in around us all the time. All told I have seen 12 so far. 2 p.m.—Sea very smooth today and a beautiful sky; one of the warmest days we have had. Can see many fish from the deck as they play around in the sea. Our guard cruiser Rochester turned back to N.Y. as soon as we picked up the escort of torpedo boats. Sea smooth and glassy in p.m.

March 25:

Sea quiet. A periscope was sighted this a.m. and transport Henderson fired at it. Our fleet broke up this p.m. The Mallory and Pocohontas are going to some other port.

When she received this letter, Annie wrote at the top "The first letter".

At Sea in the Atlantic

Dear Mamma & Nellie,

This is our eighth day at sea and I will give you a short description of our voyage so far. The night we left the harbor it was raining as it did most of the day and so far about half of the time it has been coming, just a slow drizzling rain with some flurries of snow, but taking everything into consideration, time of year, etc., I guess we have had very fair weather.

All but a couple of days when we were in the Gulf Stream it has been quite chilly but I have spent a good deal of the time on the top deck. We are on a vessel a little over five hundred feet long. It is an all-steel boat and I think we are on a very good vessel. The sea has been very smooth most of the time but several days the waves have been rolling 20 to 30 feet high. Now and then they break over the side, giving all they hit a good wetting.

It is hard to get used to the continual rolling and pitching of the boat. It rolls from side to side so that one side will be from two to 15 feet higher than the other. When the big rolls come it is hard to sit on a chair. The vessel will pitch from end to end so that one end will be 25 feet higher than the other, but that does not bother very much. The first day out the water had a kind of a green tinge, but after we got out farther it turned to a darker blue color, and when the waves break and the sun shines through the mist it is certainly pretty. It has such a pretty blue-green color. Just wish the weather was not so rough so we could be out on the top deck more.

Sea gulls were following the boat until yesterday but since then I have not seen a one. They just seem to keep flying all the time but I guess they must light in the water and swim and rest now and then.

There is quite a number of officers and men on this boat and most of them were sick the first few days out and it was funny to see them walk to the side of the boat and see how far out they could reach, but I have never felt better in my life than I have since coming on this boat. It was hard for me to get used to the roll of the vessel, especially at night but I don't mind that at all now. I sure thought I would get seasick, but so far no signs and I have been eating three squares a day...

We have passed several sailing vessels the last few days. They were tramp steamers so they told us. I am lying down and using my leg for a table so if you have trouble reading this, don't blame me too much. It is no easy matter to write that way. There is no writing desk in any of these staterooms. People can say what they want to about these sea voyages but they are not very enjoyable to me. The first few days are all right but then it gets monotonous and gets tiresome. There is nothing you can do but lay around and read or go up on deck and look around and it's the same thing all the time.

Did you ever finish that sweater you started for me Xmas? Wish you would send it as soon as I give you my address over there. It may come in handy. I told Gussie she could knit me one, but you know an extra one or two won't hurt.

Today is a beautiful day and it is fine up on deck and I have been there since early this a.m. It is about two p.m. now. The sea is very nice and quiet. The day is warm and the sea is certainly pretty. I know you would enjoy seeing it.

I have noticed a good many schools of fishes swimming about the vessel and some of them are several feet long. The water is so clear. I believe we are getting nearer to land because the sea looks lighter in color to me.

I am keeping a diary and I will tell you more about it when I come back to good old U.S.A. Arrived at a French port this a.m. I was sure glad to see land I can truthfully say. We are now in the harbor waiting to unload and I will mail this letter just as soon as I can.

Two submarine periscopes were seen by the lookout but that was all, and all I can say is I don't blame them for not coming in sight because the ships are too well escorted. Well I will write more later. Will close so bye bye.

Lovingly, Harry

Diary entries:

March 26:

Land was sighted about 7 a.m., i.e., a lighthouse, and about 9 we sighted another periscope but did not get a shot at it. Wind was very cold as we came in harbor. We dropped anchor about 1 mile from dock and unloaded part of the cargo onto tugs. Went to bed early. We were allowed to take our clothes off.

March 27:

In dock, Brest, France, and watched them unload. Put in part of the morning entertaining some French women and children in rowboats by throwing them money. Went uptown in the afternoon and drank some wine and champagne and ate supper. The streets are very narrow and the town is very hilly.

March 28:

Raining in the morning. Came to town in the afternoon and stopped at Hotel Des Voyageure and attended a show. Orders came telling us to leave Saturday.

March 29:

In Brest trying to speak French.

CHAPTER IV

SOMEWHERE IN FRANCE

When Lt. Hunt arrived in France, the following telegram was sent to his mother:
"ARRIVED SAFELY IN FRANCE. HARRY."

He wrote a four-page letter to his mother and sister on stationery with the heading:

National War Work Council
YOUNG MEN'S CHRISTIAN ASSOCIATIONS
Of the United States
"With the Colors"

Dear Mamma & Nellie,

We came on shore yesterday and I am now staying at a hotel here in town, but will leave here tomorrow for_____. Mailed you a letter yesterday and if nothing happens you should have it sometime in April. How goes everything at home and how is this old world treating you?

I never felt better in my life and am having a very enjoyable time, considering everything. Very few of the natives can talk American and as I can't speak French we have a hard time getting around but I hope to know more French by-and-by.

The weather here is cool and it was raining most of yesterday. We have had enough rain to last for some time now I think, so it might as well slack up a little. You know it rained about half the time while we were on the boat.

We were on the water just twelve days and it was sure a lonesome trip. I was certainly glad the morning we sighted land. We saw the land about three hours before we got in port. The first day in port we could not get off the boat. The harbor was just full of ships, all kinds and all sizes from the small fishing boat to the large transport and battleship. Saw several submarines sailing around the harbor, and they were queer-looking boats.

It is sure amusing the way people do things and dress over here. All of the poorer class of people wear wooden shoes, both men and women, boys and girls. They certainly make enough racket walking on the pavement. Most everyone I have seen is dressed in black due to the nation being in mourning. The stores are mostly run by women, old men and boys. You see very few young men unless they are in uniform, but you see a good many French soldiers and sailors on the streets.

The streets are very narrow, from 20 to 30 feet wide and the sidewalks are about four feet wide. The people walk mostly in the street. The streetcars are smaller than in Manhattan and have little narrow tracks, which are usually located on the side of the street. Very few automobiles but guess most of them are being used up at the Front. More horses and carts here than at home and the wagons are mostly two-wheeled affairs. They hitch the horses in tandem style. I guess the streets are too narrow to hitch them abreast.

There was a bunch of American Negro soldiers (stevedores) at the harbor to help unload the freight. They were certainly a happy bunch and they sure can put some freight in those vessels. They load the bottom or hold of the vessel with the cargo and they can certainly put in a large amount.

We got our American money changed into French money at the Y.M.C.A. and the French money is sure queer-looking stuff but I am learning its value very fast. Living expenses are cheaper here than at home but I don't like it as well but I guess that is natural.

I don't have the least idea when I will get your letters and I am told it may be a month before I get located and they find me, but just keep on writing. I suppose you received the telegram I left in the U.S. for you. I can't send cables from here but as soon as the boat arrives here it is wired across and then the messages are sent out.

This is all for this time so will close so write soon.
Lovingly, Harry
American Expeditionary Forces
Unassigned

Diary entries:

March 30:
>   Left Brest 2:10 p.m. (14:10) for Blois.

March 31:
>   Arrived Blois 6 a.m. and were taken to Caserne and quartered there.

April 1:
>   In Blois and was put to drilling and attending lectures.

April 2:
>   Same.

Somewhere in France
4/2/18
Dear Mamma and Nellie,

I am now at_____ and like it very much better than I did at _____ where we landed. We stayed there about three days and then came up to this burg. It is about 600 kilometers (350 miles).

We were on the train about 20 hours, including all night, with very little sleep. The coaches here are very small and also the engine and we would almost be afraid to ride on such trains in the good old U.S.A. Each train is made up of first, second, and third class passengers and the L—d knows the first is poor enough. The coaches are divided up into compartments and each compartment has an outside door but I guess they could be worse.

At the railroad eating houses the first thing they bring you is a bottle of beer and some wine. You know the French are great after the wine but I can't do very much for it and the beer is not much.

One thing that attracts my attention here more than anything else is the small narrow streets and their crooked course. Of course, when you take into consideration that some of the buildings have been standing for several hundred years and the towns were laid out even before America was discovered, it is no wonder they are as they are.

Saw a chateau (castle) that they started to build 45 years before Christ. It was used by Julius Caesar at one time as his headquarters. There are many other chateaus around here and I want to go through them if I get the chance, but don't know how long we will get to stay here, as this place is just a kind of a clearing house.

We are quartered in an old French army quarters and we have fairly good quarters considering everything. We are located just on the edge of town and after four o'clock we can go where we want to put in the rest of the time, in drilling and listening to lectures. They drill all the officers in one company and it is just the thing for us because you know about how long I have been on the road traveling and lying around. We are a long ways from the Front here and don't know much if any more about how the present battle is going than you folks do, but the present dope is that the Germans are being held, and being driven back at some points.

Spring is here and everything is nice and green and there is lots of garden truck coming into town. The people here are a much better class than in the town we landed in, and this is a much cleaner town, which helps a whole lot.

They can say what they want to about the French girls but I have seen very few that I would call good-looking. I don't think they compare with the American girls, especially one I know.

I don't have the least idea when I will get your letters. One officer told me today that he has been here almost four months and received his first mail today, but when I do get it, it will certainly be welcomed. It is very nice here today and I am feeling fine. How is everything with you and how is this old world treating you?

There are many things of interest I would like to tell you about but will have to wait until I see you. Will close as I have another letter to write so bye-bye and write soon.

Lovingly, Harry
A.E.F., Unassigned

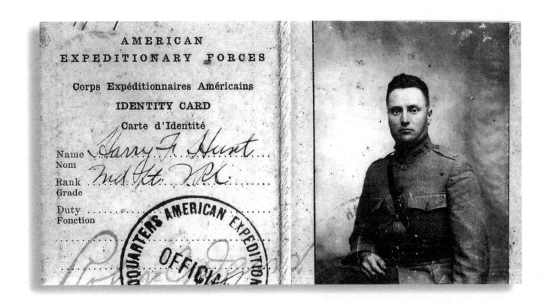

USS Crane, Destroyer 109, built at Union Iron Works, San Francisco, WWI. This picture was taken in April, 1919, Hudson River and 96th Street, New York, on return of the USS Crane from Brest.
(Photo courtesy of The Arizona Historical Society/ Tucson, 42102)

AMERICAN AVIATOR AND HIS FRENCH INSTRUCTOR INSPECTING BATTLE PLANE.   SERIES NO. 12   222668

Firing the 14-inch gun.
Notice how the gun rises above the wall to fire.

in France   Harry Hunt
                             1918

Mud Hollow,
Epinonville, Meuse-
Argonne offensive,
10/16/1918 Troops of the
356th Infantry, 89th Div.
in background advancing to relieve
32nd., Div. night of the 17th.,
314th Field Signal Batallion in
foreground.

ORDER OF BATTLE

OF THE

UNITED STATES LAND FORCES

IN THE

WORLD WAR

AMERICAN EXPEDITIONARY FORCES

DIVISIONS

Prepared in the Historical Section
Army War College

UNITED STATES
GOVERNMENT PRINTING OFFICE
WASHINGTON : 1931

For sale by the Superintendent of Documents, Washington, D. C. - - Price $1.50 (Buckram)

35th DIVISION (NG)
COMPOSITION

69th Infantry Brigade	70th Infantry Brigade	60th Field Artillery Brigade
137th Infantry	139th Infantry	128th Field Artillery (75)
138th Infantry	140th Infantry	129th Field Artillery (75)
120th Machine Gun Battalion	130th Machine Gun Battalion	130th Field Artillery (155)
		110th Trench Mortar Battery

Divisional Troops	Trains
128th Machine Gun Battalion	110th Train Headquarters and Military Police
110th Engineers	110th Ammunition Train
110th Field Signal Battalion	110th Supply Train
Headquarters Troop	110th Engineer Train
	110th Sanitary Train (Ambulance Companies and Field Hospitals 137-140)

ATTACHED

Fr 80th Territorial Inf	Gérardmer Sector, Aug 14–Sept 2, 1918.
1st Aero Sq 2d Bln Co Fr 219th FA (75) Fr 1st and 2d Bns 247th FA (75) one bn Fr 451st Arty (105) Fr 3d Bn 317th Arty (155) Fr 4th and 5th Bns 282d Arty (220) one sq Fr 2d Cav one bn 53d Pion Inf 344th Tank Bn (less one co)	at times during Meuse-Argonne Operation, between Sept 26 and Oct 1, 1918.

DETACHED

60th FA Brig and 110th Am Tn	at Angers and Camp Coëtquidan, June 9–Aug 14, 1918, with 1st Div in Meuse-Argonne Operation, Oct 1–2; with 81st Div in Meuse-Argonne Operation, Nov 7–11; in Sommedieue Area, Nov 12–Dec 18, 1918.
60th FA Brig (less 110th TM Btry) and 110th Am Tn	in Sommedieue Area, Dec 19, 1918–Jan 22, 1919
110th TM Btry	at Preigney, Villevêque, Angers, and St-Nazaire, Dec 19, 1918–April 19, 1919.
110th Engrs and Tn	at Brest, Feb 8–Apr 11, 1919.

87th DIVISION (NA)

COMPOSITION

173d Infantry Brigade	174th Infantry Brigade	162d Field Artillery Brigade
345th Infantry 346th Infantry 335th Machine Gun Battalion	347th Infantry 348th Infantry 336th Machine Gun Battalion	334th Field Artillery (75) 335th Field Artillery (75) 336th Field Artillery (155) 312th Trench Mortar Battery

Divisional Troops	Trains
334th Machine Gun Battalion 312th Engineers 312th Field Signal Battalion Headquarters Troop	312th Train Headquarters and Military Police 312th Ammunition Train 312th Supply Train 312th Engineer Train 312th Sanitary Train (Ambulance Companies and Field Hospitals 345–348)

DETACHED

345th Inf	with Intermediate Section and Base Section No 1, SOS, Sept to Dec, 1918.
346th Inf	with Base Section No 1, SOS, Sept, 1918, to March, 1919.
347th Inf	with Intermediate Section, SOS, Sept to Dec, 1918.
348th Inf	with Base Section No 2, SOS, Sept, 1918, to Feb, 1919.
334th MG Bn 335th MG Bn 336th MG Bn	with Base Section No 1, SOS, Sept, 1918, to Feb, 1919.
162d FA Brig and 312th Am Tn	with Base Sections Nos 2 and 7, and Intermediate Section, SOS, Sept, 1918, to Feb, 1919.
312th Engrs and Tn	with Base Sections Nos 2 and 7, SOS, Sept, 1918, to June, 1919.
312th Sup Tn	with Base Section No 1, SOS, Sept, 1918, to July, 1919.
312th F Sig Bn	with Base Section No 1, SOS, Sept, 1918 to March, 1919.
312th Sn Tn	with Base Sections Nos 1 and 2, and Intermediate Section, SOS, Sept, 1918, to January, 1919.

AMERICAN EXPEDITIONARY FORCES
HEADQUARTERS   SERVICES OF SUPPLY.

April 4, 1918.

SPECIAL ORDERS)

NO. 23.

Extract.

73.   Upon recommendation of the Chief Quartermaster
Second Lieutenant Harry F. Hunt, V. R. C., now casually at
Blois, will proceed to Bourbonne-les-Bains, reporting upon
arrival to the Commanding Officer, Remount Depot, for assignment to duty.

          The travel directed is necessary in the military
service:

          By Command of Major General Kernan:

                              Johnson Hagood,
                              Chief of Staff

OFFICIAL

    L. H. Bash,
    Adjutant General.

A true copy

Paul F. Mann

Paul F. Mann,
1st Lt. FA NG

SPECIAL REGULATIONS NO. 70

REGULATIONS

GOVERNING THE

Army Veterinary Service

WASHINGTON
GOVERNMENT PRINTING OFFICE
1918

Somewhere in France
Sunday, April 7, 1918

This is Sunday evening and as there are a few things of interest I will tell you about them. I have been at this camp about a week and everything is going just fine with very little to complain about. France is sure a queer place compared to our good old U.S.A. The people here are about 100 years behind the times and it's sure amusing the way they do things.

We were excused from all duties yesterday afternoon and I went to town. As it was market day it was quite amusing to watch the different conveyances that were used to bring the produce to market. You could see the push carts, dog-drawn carts, and horse-drawn carts and the various carts were all sizes and descriptions. Some of the horse-drawn carts had wheels that were six to seven feet high, the largest wheels I have ever seen. They certainly put some loads on these large two-wheeled carts. You will see some old woman pushing a cart and a dog latched to it pulling when he feels like it. From general appearance the dog doesn't feel like pulling very often but he can guard the cart when the woman goes away. You can't even make friends with the dogs over here. I guess they can't tell whether you are scolding them or trying to be friendly.

I went through an old chateau (castle) here the other day that was partially built during the thirteenth century, and the different rulers after that added to it as they saw fit and to suit their own fancy. It was a very interesting place and of course they had a whole lot of dope to tell us about it, when certain kings did so and so, etc. Would like to tell you more about it, but if I told you too much you might learn where I am and that is against regulations, you know.

Very little of the furniture was remaining, but in one part that is now used as a museum there were many pretty pictures. The architectural designs were simply great, better by far than anything we see in our modern buildings. Of course plainness is used more at this time.

I have seen quite a number of aeroplanes flying about camp but I think they are from the aero training camp. I have been trying to pick up a little of the French language but so far I have not succeeded very well. They have so many silent letters in words and their pronunciation is so different, but I guess it is up to us to learn it as very few of the French can talk English.

The bread eaten by the French people is made from rye and I believe they make the largest loaves I have ever seen, three and four feet long and eight to fifteen inches in diameter, and they never think of wrapping it up, just carry it along under their arms. You see women who are well-dressed shopping with fishnet bags. They will buy eggs and just put them in loose in the bag and go ahead about their shopping.

I sent you a souvenir handkerchief the other day which you should have by the

25

time you get this letter.

I don't think the letters that are sent from the U.S. to American soldiers over here are censored. An officer here censors his own mail, but his letters can be re-censored. But you know when you are put on your honor to do a thing, you must do that.

The French laundries here are very odd. They have a large boat on a stream and wash the clothes there and rinse them in the river and when it has been raining as it is here and the streams are up I don't see how they can get them very clean.

As I must write another letter tonight and as I have told you all I know will close so write soon.

Lovingly, Harry

Diary entries:

April 2 to 9:

In Blois. quartered at the Caserne. Went through chateau at Blois while here. Order away on Tuesday, April 9.

April 10:

Enroute traveling on train and arrived at Bourbonne Les Bains. Stayed at Hotel DeCommerce.

April 11:

Was assigned to remount depot. Got a permanent billet and was assigned to it in the Hotel Des Sources. Watched them (Amex) unload horses and mules and brand them.

April 12:

Picked out a bay saddle horse and attended to a few duties.

From "Veterinary Military History of the United States", by Merillat and Campbell, Vol. II, page 695:

"Inspection of Bourbonne les Bains.—The first advance remount depot established was at Bourbonne les Bains, a beautiful spa among the scenery of that ancient habitation. The depot was a tragedy from the start. It was at an unwisely chosen location. The clay soil is from three to four feet deep and it was kept soaked with an unusual rainfall..."

From "Final Report of Gen. John J. Pershing, Commander-in Chief, American Expeditionary Forces," Washington Government Printing Office, 1920. Pages 65-66:

"As far as the regulating officer was concerned, supplies were divided into four main classes. The first class constituted food, forage and fuel, needed and consumed every day; the second, uniforms, shoes, blankets and horse shoes, which wear out with reasonable regularity; the third, articles of equipment which require replacement at irregular intervals, such as rolling kitchens, rifles and escort wagons; the fourth class covered articles, the flow of which depended upon tactical operations, such as ammunition and construction material. Articles in the first class were placed on an automatic basis, but formal requisition was eliminated as far as possible for all classes."

From "Final Report of Gen. John J. Pershing, Commander-in Chief, American Expeditionary Forces," Washington Government Printing Office, 1920. Pages 70-71:

REMOUNTS.

"13. The shortage of animals was a serious problem throughout the war. In July, 1917, the French agreed to furnish our forces with 7,000 animals a month, and accordingly the War Department was requested to discontinue shipments. On August 24, however, the French advised us that it would be impossible to furnish the number of animals originally stated, and Washington was again asked to supply animals, but none could be sent over until November, and then only a limited number.

"Early in 1918, after personal intervention and much delay, the French Government made requisition on the country, and we were able to obtain 50,000 animals. After many difficulties, the Purchasing Board was successful in obtaining permission, in the summer of 1918, to export animals from Spain, but practically no animals were received until after the Armistice.

"Every effort was made to reduce animal requirements—by increased motorization of artillery and by requiring mounted officers and men to walk—but in spite of all these efforts, the situation as to animals grew steadily worse. The shortage by November exceeded 106,000, or almost one-half of all our needs. To relieve the crisis in this regard, during the Meuse-Argonne battle, Marshal Foch requisitioned 13,000 animals from the French Armies and placed them at my disposal."

From "Veterinary Military History of the United States," Vol. II, by Merillat and Campbell, page 779:

"...the proper place for the mobile veterinary section was in advance of the headquarters, among the trains and in action just behind the artillery where the casualties were to be expected and where it could cooperate with the corps and army in making evacuations...."

CHAPTER V

"A STRANGER IN A STRANGE LAND"

Somewhere in France
April 14, 1918
Dear Mamma & Nellie,

"A stranger in a strange land," you know I used to use that expression when I wrote when I was on trips, but now I am certainly a stranger in a strange land. It seems that way, too, because everyplace I go I hear a lingo that I cannot understand and I am not learning it very fast either, but as yet I have not tried very hard, but intend to by-and-by.

I am a couple of hundred miles from where I last wrote you. Came here Wednesday and was on the train about twenty-four hours making the journey. I am now located at _____ and I am assigned to duty to an advancement, that is, I am in what is called the advance section and I can't tell you any more.

A remount station is where large numbers of horses and mules are kept and we supply them to the Front, as it is called, as they need them up there. I have been kept pretty busy as you know there is lots of work around anything that is just starting and we have a good many sick ones on hand at present. While I am kept pretty busy I enjoy the work and it makes the time pass more rapidly.

There is a good bunch of officers here and everything is going just fine. I am located in a small town of four to five thousand but it is a very pretty town and the surrounding country is very pretty, but the people and the way they live and do things is very amusing. The poor class especially. Their houses consist of one large building (of course varying in size) and they will have the barn in one end and the house in the other, and where the houses are built close together one door will be to the house and the other to the barn of the adjoining building, and this warm weather you can imagine the smell. In the summertime the flies must be pretty

29

thick. But the French do not pay much attention to sanitation.

Their wagons etc. are comical affairs and they will string three and four horses (tandem style) to one wagon where if they would hitch them as we do, one team would be plenty. Of course their wagons are all heavy, handmade affairs, and are awkward and pull heavy. Their plows and other farming implements are just about 100 years behind the times. Very few French automobiles but that is due a whole lot I imagine to the war, they are being used at the Front, and the great scarcity of gasoline and coal oil.

I am now billeted (rooming) in a hotel that was set aside for the U.S.A. and I have a very good room and a good bed. The room is furnished by the government but I must take care of it or have it done so I pay the people here a franc, a little less than 18 cents a day, to take care of it. They furnish me towels, clean and polish my shoes and furnish the bedding and everything, but I am too lazy to do it for that money and this way I always have a nice clean room.

I am boarding with one of the companies of soldiers and we have plenty of good substantial food and you know that is what is required. There are several other officers there and we eat by ourselves and buy a few extra things as we want them. So you see that I am not suffering any. The town is always kept dark at night and I am using a candle to illuminate my room.

Aeroplanes are very numerous around here, that is, flying over. Saw eight in one (bunch, flock, herd) or squadron as they may be called but they were flying so high you could not tell very much about them.

I have a fine large bay horse I am riding now and I don't believe I ever rode a horse I liked as well. I am enjoying some good horseback rides and the country about here is beautiful. So much of it is wooded and the ground is quite hilly. You can see fields right up on top and the sides of the hills and it is very pretty. The fields are pretty and green and are just as neat as lawns are in the U.S.

We don't know any more about the present battle that is now raging than you do because about all the news we get is from an American paper printed in this country and you get the same. Men coming from the Front only know about their particular section and that is not very much in this war.

I have plenty of other paper but thought I would use this up first. Mamma, how is everything and how is this old world treating you? Have not received a bit of mail since arriving here and don't hardly expect to for a week or two. It takes a long time for it to get around. Will close so good night and write soon.

Lovingly, Harry

Address me thus: Lieut. Harry F. Hunt V.R.C.

American E.F.

France

And be sure to put the V.R.C. after my name.

France
4-19-18
Dear Mamma & Sister,

This has been a very cold day and it was trying hard to snow this morning, but it did not last long, and thank goodness it did warm up a little this p.m. It certainly has been cool and damp here since I last wrote and has been raining about half the time, just a slow drizzling rain, the kind that makes it disagreeable. It sure is nice to be out in, and I have the pleasure of being out in most of it, too.

Of all the muddy places I have ever seen this place is the worst. It certainly is tiresome wading mud, and while I ride horseback to the different corrals, I have to get off there. I have no rubber boots but intend to get a pair the first chance I get. In the meantime I am wearing my hightop shoes, which answer the purpose very well.

Was sure pleased yesterday when I received five letters from the dear old U.S.A., two from you and three from Gussie, and every one of them was welcomed as they are the first mail I had received since landing in France. One of your letters was the one you sent to me at Hoboken and one of Gussie's was the same. Not bad at all was it, because I have only been in France a little over three weeks and I think from now on mail will come more regular. You should have received several letters from me before now. I have written one or two letters a week ever since I have landed and will try to write at least once a week whether I hear from you or not. I think with the mail service that is in force over here now you will hear regularly from me. The only thing is my letters will be just a little longer on the way.

I am still at this advance remount station and at present we are kept pretty busy. We are receiving and sending out large numbers of horses and mules all the time.

I believe I have told you about everything of interest that has happened since my leaving the U.S. and so far everything has went just lovely and I am feeling just fine, only I can't get on to the way these French people do things. They are so far behind the times.

Since coming here I have seen where the large German Zeppelin L49 was brought down last August 20th. If you can find where it was brought down you will know one place I have been. Wish I could tell you more, but I can't, and it is very hard to write when so many things can't be spoken about. Wish I could meet some of my old friends over here. While there are a good many here, I know it would just be chance luck if I would meet them, as American troops are scattered all over France. Everyplace I have been I have seen American soldiers, and while my friends may be in the next town I have no way of finding it out.

In regards to that bank account at Little Rock, I don't think there is a cent there. I drew out every bit of my money. But for fear I might have overdrawn I simply gave them your address and name and my bank book and told them if things did not

31

come out even to draw on you. Have you heard from Frank Pedroja as yet?

And so my little sister has just commenced to realize that college days are not so unpleasant after all. Just let me say that this old world is a good old world and there are many ups and downs but just keep a stiff upper lip and keep smiling and everything will come out allright. I would think there would be quite a number of jobs open as so many boys are away and I imagine there will be a good many more before long. Must close and write to someone else so good night and write soon.

Lovingly, Harry
American E.F. France
A.P.O. 720 (American Post Office explanatory)
Just add this A.P.O. 720 to my address.

"With the Colors" Y.M.C.A.

France
4/25/18
Dear Mamma and Nellie,

This is the end of another rainy day but that is about the only kind of weather we ever have here it seems. Since the eleventh of this month I think it has only missed one day, rain every other day and the mud is a fright. I have seen mud in many different places and different kinds of mud, but this country certainly takes the premium. Just wish you could have some of this rain and we could have some of your drouth, cause this rainy, muddy weather is certainly getting tiresome.

The natives here claim that the over-amount of rainfall is due to the heavy bombardment up on the Front, but anyhow we are getting enough of it.

I have at last managed to get ahold of a pair of rubber boots and I will have them tomorrow morning. They are going to help some. Sent to L— with another fellow and he got them for me.

In the corrals the mud is all the way from a couple of inches to a foot deep and it is certainly nice when you have to wade around in it. Enough about the mud and weather and will now try to write you some news, but all I can say is that it is certainly scarce.

We received quite a number of mules this morning and it was sure fun watching the men brand them. The long-eared creatures would walk slowly up past where they were heating the iron, their ears bobbing back and forth and taking life just as easy as they could, mule fashion. Then the man leading him would pat him kindly on the neck and cover his eye up. Then they would stick the branding iron up against Mr. Mule and he would immediately proceed to take on new life. Some of them proved themselves to be very good actors. When it was all over Mr. Mule would wonder what had happened. It amuses the French people very much to watch it done and you will see women of all ages, 16 to 50, and some with babies in their arms watching, quite different than in our country.

Received your letter No. 2 today and two from Gesina forwarded from Hoboken and they were all read with pleasure, but methinks you waited a little over two days for a letter. In your letter of the 27 of March you said you expected a letter in a day or so, and that day I mailed my first letter to you from this side, because it was the first chance I had had. But you should have received my telegram saying I had arrived safe.

I am feeling fine and enjoying myself as best I can but it is sorta lonesome here I can tell you. I have only been out one night and that was to a prizefight given by the soldiers here. But there is nothing else to go to.

Do you remember those hightop shoes I bought in Manhattan when I was at the serum plant, well, I had them half-soled again and hob nails put in the sole and heel so you see I am getting some good wear out of them.

Will tell Gussie to write to you but I guess the dear girl is pretty busy. What does Nellie intend to do after she finishes school? Mamma, this may seem like a short letter but it is the hardest thing I ever tried to do to write long interesting letters from over here. It is the same thing every day and so many things we can't write so will close and bid you a fond Bonne Nuit and write soon.

Lovingly, Harry

Oh yes, I am sending you a request for the sweater and cigars, which request must be put in the package according to the new P.O. regulation.

(1)

May 3, 1918

My dear little Sister and Mother,

My little sister's letter came to hand today and contents were certainly read with pleasure. This has been the first really nice day we have had here since I have been in this town, and believe me it was certainly enjoyed. Yesterday was fairly nice, only one little shower in the evening which is not bad at all.

I think it is a very good plan about numbering the letters and I will try to do so from now on, and will call this number one, but I have written seven or eight letters since arriving on this side. It seems queer to have just read your letter saying I had arrived. It seems like I have been here a long time over a month.

We came in the harbor in France March 26, landed March 27 and left the port of embarkation March 14 so you see we made very quick time considering everything, but I have told you all that dope a long time ago.

Wish I could tell you where I was etc. but you know I can't. But then keep your eyes open and your ears alert and you may learn. About all I can say is that I am in the Eastern part of France in a small town, but when I return I will tell you all.

Wish I could come and watch my little sister graduate but then you had better go ahead just the same as if I was there. From what we hear we may be over here some little time yet, but I don't know any more than I did. My opinion of this war is it may end in a few months and again it may be a few years so draw your own conclusions. It is all guesswork with me.

I met a vet here today who just came over by the name of Ray from K.S.A.C. Class of '16. I did not remember him, but he did me and I certainly enjoyed visiting with him over old times.

As it is getting late I will ring off, so Bonne Nuit and sweet dreams. Write soon.
Lovingly, Harry

(2)
A.E.F. France
May 5, 1918
My dear Mamma and Nellie,
Your good letter came to hand today and I will now proceed to answer it to the best of my ability. It has been drizzling all day here and acts as though it will keep it up most of the night. Saturday was a very pretty and warm day and the sun shone all day but last night it started to rain again.

That vet's name from K.S.A.C. is spelled Reaugh instead of Ray as I said in my last letter. Wish I could come and help you make your garden, but I might talk different if I were there, you know environment often changes our minds. Wish you would not worry so much about me getting sick etc. So far I have never felt better in my life and everything is going just lovely.

In your letter you were expecting to hear from me every day but I am making a guess that you received my first letter from over here about or between the 15th and 20th of April. Now tell me how good a guesser I am. I have not heard from Gesina for a long time. Can't imagine what is the trouble but maybe it is the postal service over here. As you say, any amount of mail is lost.

Sure wish I had those cigars, but I sent you a request for them some time ago. Nothing can be sent over here without a request. Wish you would send me a Masonic ring, just a small or medium sized one with the Square and Compass and G. (XX)...believe me I am certainly glad I am a member of that lodge.

In this request I am leaving a space and if you think you can write like I do, add something if you want to, but I have about everything I need and can get about everything here. Cigars that sell in America for ten cents each we can buy here for

34

six cents from the U.S. commissary, cigarettes cheaper than in U.S. and candy very cheap when they have it. Bought a pair of hip rubber boots the other day for $2.20 and you know that is cheap. Above all don't worry because I am feeling fine and everything is going just fine.

I sent you a couple of handmade lace collars the other day for your graduation present, and I hope you like them but if they are not style and don't fit, please let me know, also tell me how you like them. Anything you want let me know and I will try to supply your needs.

Also help yourself to that money in the bank and if it plays out I will try to send you more. Did Frank Pedroja ever send that note as I mentioned in one of my last letters from Camp Pike? Have not heard from Gesina for some time. Maybe the dear girl is sick, but I hope not.

I was out pretty close today where a German Zeppelin was brought down some time ago but it was all cleaned up and you could not see anything. Some of the men that were the first here saw it.

I am sending you a piece of paper the size I want the Masonic ring I spoke of in my letter to Nellie. I would not get a very expensive one, but at the same time get one that won't break easily. You know France is mostly Catholic and you can't buy a ring anyplace I have been.

Another officer and I intended to ride out this p.m. where a German Zeppelin was brought down some time ago but too much rain. It is only a short distance and I have been out before but he had never been out.

We are very fortunate in having a good bath house here in this town (bath - Bain house - Maison) and it is not every town in France that has such a thing. And we have plenty of hot water as it is mineral water of some kind and comes out of the ground hot. Heat of any kind is scarce here, I am telling you.

Mamma, I want you to tell me about those collars I sent to Nellie, whether they are style etc. and about what you think they are worth. I may want to send someone else some of them. Would you care for any?

Mamma, this is a very short letter I know, but it is hard to find very much to tell you. It is the same every day and very little happening that I have not already told you. So will ring off for tonight and go to snoozeland so Bonne Nuit and write soon.

Lovingly, Harry

General John J. Pershing asked the men to write to their mothers on Mother's Day. Lt. Hunt had written "Mother's letter" on the upper right-hand corner of the envelope above the postmark (U.S. Army Postal Service, May 13, 4 p.m.)

Photo courtesy Ft. Huachuca Museum

General John J. Pershing

36

(3 or 4)

May 12, 1918

My dear Mother and Sister,

This is Sunday evening and as this is Mother's Day I am going to fill the request of General Pershing that everyone write to his mother on this day. How are you today, Mother, and I wonder what you are doing. It rained here all morning but this afternoon has been pretty nice. Yesterday was a very pretty day until evening when it rained hard. But you know that is a very common occurrence over here. It has rained every day since I last wrote to you.

No mail for over a week from you but the mail service is simply punk over here. I have not heard from Gesina as yet since her first two letters came but everyone is having trouble with mail so guess all I can do is to wait patiently. But here is hoping I won't have to wait much longer.

This country must be agreeing with me. I got weighed yesterday and tipped the scales at 196 pounds. I have never felt better in my life, only for a little cold I had last week but I am over or about over it now. But you know it is natural for a person to have colds now and then.

I went to a movie show last Wednesday night entitled "They're Off" given by the Amer. Y.M.C.A. and enjoyed it very much. Also took in a boxing contest one night between some of the Amer. troops stationed here. We only get to see a movie show about every two weeks and believe me it helps to break the monotony.

I read an article in the paper the other day where they thought the U.S. Gov. would give commutation of quarters to officers' wives, children or dependent parents and if they do I am going to put in for you. With my present rank you will be entitled to $24.00 a month. You might just as well have it as not, so don't be surprised if you get a check for that amount some of these days, but don't be surprised if you don't. You never can tell what is going to happen. If it does pass they will commence paying it from April 16, 1918, as that is when the Bill passed, but the controller of the treasury has not acted on it. Sure hope it passes, don't you?

Bought some good candy from the commissary yesterday; come and see me and I will let you sample it. We can buy extra-good quality chocolate in a one-pound tin box for fifty cents (Amer. money) and it sure tastes good. I am getting to be a regular kid for candy. As this is all I think of will close so good night, and write soon.

Lovingly, Harry
OK Harry F. Hunt
2nd Lt. V.R.C.

(3 o 4)

Some Where in France.
3/12/18

My dear Mother and Sister, This is Sunday evening and as this mothers day I am going to fill the request of General Pershing that every one write to their mother on this day, How are you today mother and Levonda what you are doing, It rained here all morning but this afternoon has been pretty nice. Yesterday was a very pretty day until evening when it rained hard, But you know that is a very common occurance over here cause it has rained every day since I last wrote to you. No mail for over a week from you but the mail service is simply punk over here and I have not heard from Lesure as yet since her first two letters came but every one is having trouble with mail so I guess all I can do is to wait patiently but here is hoping I won't have to wait much longer. This country must be agreeing with me cause I got weighted yesterday and tiped the scales at one hundred and ninety six pounds and I have never felt better in my life, only for a little cold I had last week but I am over it about over it now. But then you know it is natural for a person to have cold now and then, I went to a movie show last Wednesday

2

might entitled "them off" given by the Amer. Y.M.
C.A. and enjoyed it very much. Also took in a boxing
contest one night between some of the Army troops
stationed here. We only get to see a movie show here
about every two weeks and believe me it helps to break
the monotony. I read an article in the paper the other
day where they thought the U.S. Gov. would give commutation
of quarters to officers wives, children or dependent parents and
if they do I am going to put in for you, cause with my
present rank you will be entitled to twenty four dollars a month
and you might just as well have it as not, so don't be surprised
if you get a check for that amount some of these days,
but don't be surprised if you don't get it cause you
never can tell what is going to happen, but if it does pass
they will commence paying it from (April 16 1918) cause that
is when the bill passed but the controller of the treasury has
not acted on it. Sure hope it passes don't you. Bought some
good candy from the commissary yesterday come and
see me and I will let you sample it. We can buy extra
good quality chocolates in one pound tin box for
fifty cents (Amer. money) and it sure tastes good. I am
getting to be a regular kid for candy. As this is all
I think of I will close so good night and write soon
                              Lovingly Harry

OK
Harry H. Hunt
2 nd Lt O.R.C.

No. 4 or 5. Can't keep the numbers straight but will write every week so you can tell that way. But will try numbering this one No. 4.

Somewhere in France

May 19, 1918

My dear Mamma and Nellie,

This is Sunday evening once more and it has been one beautiful day. It has been clear and the sun has shone very hot and we have had beautiful weather all week. It only rained one day and very little that day, and believe me it certainly seems good to have some nice bright days after so much wet weather. Although this evening it is clouding up and acts very much like it is going to rain.

I was over to _____ last Monday in a car and did a little shopping so to speak. Four of us drove over in an Army car and I enjoyed the trip very much. It is about 35 miles from here and it took us less than an hour to drive back, thanks to the good roads which this country has.

The scenery is very pretty. Everything is so neat and green and there are so many villages and they look very pretty from a distance. The buildings are all white stone with red tile roofs. You hardly ever see a frame building of any kind here, but I guess fire has taught the people that they could not build frame buildings and live as they do here.

Received your letter No. five yesterday and the contents were certainly read with pleasure. That certainly must have been some class scrap, I guess the canning factory of the faculty will have to get busy now and do their spring canning???

Where does Nellie's man go for training and is it an officers' training camp that he is going to? Things must be different in the States than they were some time ago. But I knew the time was coming when the people would look at things differently.

We are daily expecting to hear of another big German drive, but they don't seem to be ready. But methinks they realize now that their game is up, but we will still have to show them first.

Wish I could come and help you eat strawberries. I have seen a few plants here and they are just in bloom and perhaps we may have some berries by-and-by.

I saw an officer the other day who knows Lester Stryker and told me where Lester was, but I can't tell you.

Does this new draft law take Gene in? I suppose Jennie will be worried, but then I suppose it is natural for mothers to worry, is it not, Mamma, but I don't think they should. As a rule it is easier on the boys than it is on their parents. You know it is sure some trip etc. and I know you would enioy it very much. Mamma, this is all I think of now so will ring off and bid thee a fond Bonne Nuit good night, so write soon.

Lovingly, Harry

France, 25 May '18.

SPECIAL ORDERS)

NO.   115)

1.   In compliance with telegraphic instructions from Headquarters A.S.S.O.S., dated May 25th 1918, 2nd Lieutenant Harry L. Hunt, V.R.C., in charge, and a detachment of twenty (20) enlisted men 3rd Cavalry, and one (1) man Quartermaster Corps, will proceed by truck to Prauthoy. Upon arrival thereat Lieutenant Hunt will report to Lieutenant H. M. Savage, V.C., and take over sixty (60) animals from Lieutenant Savage and return with his detachment and sixty (60) animals to Remount Depot, A.P.O. 720.

The Quartermaster Corps will furnish the necessary transportation and travel rations for twenty one (21) men for three (3) days. Any unused rations will be turned in to the Quartermaster upon completion of the journey.

The travel directed is necessary in the military service.

x   x   x

By order of MAJOR SPRING:

A. P. THAYER,

Captain, 3rd Cavalry,
Adjutant.

APT/OHS

Lt N F Hunt, NRC.
GPO 720 A.E.F.   May 12.   Mothers letter

                                    U.S. ARMY
                                    MAY 13
                                    4 PM   720
                                    POSTAL SERVICE
                                              1918

        A.E.F. PASSED AS CENSORED 966
                                    Mrs Annie L Hunt
                                    1010 Bluemont ave
                                    Manhattan
                                        Kansas
    O.K.   United States of Amer
    Harry H Hunt
    2nd Lt NRC.

Address me this way
Lieut. Harry F. Hunt
Veterinary Reserve Corps
American E.F.
A.P.O. 720

France
May 29, 1918
Dear Mamma and Nellie,

This is a very cool evening here and it has been cool the past few days, but thank goodness we are having no rain. Almost two weeks now without a rain, and I believe this country is really what we have so often heard it called, Sunny France.

Returned from about a 100 mile trip yesterday evening and was one tired boy. I went after a bunch of horses but they were not what I wanted so did not bring them back. I took the trip overland in trucks and had twenty-one men with me. We sure saw some beautiful country and some very interesting sights.

We went through an old town said to be one of the oldest in France and it was very picturesque. The fortifications around it were very interesting to me. It was surrounded by a high wall and just outside of the wall was a deep ditch. We went into the town through gates which were just large openings in through the walls and a drawbridge was left down from this opening in the wall to make the bridge, so in case of attack the gate could be closed. You know you often see pictures of fortified towns like this. Wish we were allowed to take pictures over here but nothing doing. I would sure like to have a few pictures of the things here so I could show them to you when I return.

Received a whole lot of mail just before I left on the trip. Several letters from you and a few others but none from Gussie. Received one from Marie Van Horn in Wichita (you know the girl who was married last year and they are our best pals there) and she said Gussie was allright and was writing and I can't understand why I don't receive the letters. Your letters were the first you wrote since hearing from me over here and they were sure welcomed and read with pleasure.

I am sorry to hear my little sister is not going to get her diploma. Can she finish this summer? I am glad you liked the handkerchief that was mailed after I had been over here a week.

This is all tonight, Mamma. I am too tired to write more now cause I am certainly being kept busy. So goodnight and write soon.

Lovingly, Harry

France
6/3/18
My dear Mamma and Nellie,

Your letter and commencement announcement received a couple of days ago, also two letters from Gesina and believe me they were all welcomed. The two from Gussie were the first I had received in over a month. Can't imagine where all her other letters are. She said she had been writing right along but that is the way over here, the mail certainly gets balled up at times.

We are still having fine weather here and I am enjoying it, but a good rain now would be beneficial to the country. I am enclosing a money order in this letter for ($100.00) one hundred dollars that I want you to keep for me unless you need it. I have paid up my liberty bond contract so you should receive them some of these days. I had until August to pay for the bonds but thought I might just as well pay for them now as I had the money. When you get them change them, for the last issue because the last issue pays more interest.

Did you ever receive the letter I wrote you from Camp Pike just before I left in regard to what I told Frank Pedroja at Lincoln, Ks. to do. You have never mentioned it in any of your letters that I have received. I am being kept very busy here now but the work is interesting and I enjoy it. It helps to make the time pass more rapidly, and believe me it passes slow enough.

Would sure like to get some pictures over here but at present there is nothing doing but as you say when things are more settled I guess they will allow us to. The commencement invitation is very pretty and I thank my little sister for it. Wonder if you have received the present—collars I sent. I want you to tell me if they are in style in the U.S. etc. You know I don't know very much about such things.

Some of the troops here are giving a minstrel show this week and I want to go tomorrow night. This is all I can think of so will close so good night and write soon.

Lovingly, Harry

France Somewhere
June 17, 1918
Dear Mamma & Nellie,

This is the end of another rainy day and it is just a little bit cool tonight. A fire would come in very handy I can tell you, but we have none. It started to rain hard last night and kept it up until about noon today, but we needed the rain and I only hope it clears off and stays nice again. How are you these days and how is this old world treating you?

I never felt better in my life. I tip the sales at almost 200 pounds, without a blouse on, and I am riding about ten miles every day horseback.

My Ingersol watch went dead on me last night and I am now wearing a French wristwatch. Paid forty-six francs for it ($5.71). It has a phosporescent dial and I like it real well so far. Just hope that it keeps good time.

Received a very good letter from Ray O yesterday and one from the serum company in Wichita, the only mail I have received in over ten days. There is sure one ball-up on mail over here. Ray is still in Texas but thinks they will come over here very soon. But that's what they all think and you never can tell how soon you are coming.

Mr. Cory said he wanted me back at the serum plant and to hurry and get the Kaiser because they need me and need me bad. I am glad they feel that way. My services must have been satisfactory.

I can't understand where Gussie's letters go. I only receive one out of about ten, but you know such is life...I wonder if Nellie received the package I sent her for graduation, but of course I have not had time to hear about it. Hope she enjoys wearing them.

Too cold and no news so will close and go to bed. Good night and write soon.
Lovingly, Harry

Diary entry:

June 22

Left Bourbonne Les Bains for Chatillon Sur Seine and will be in Chatillon Sur Seine until August 11.

COPY OF TELEGRAM
RECIEVED.

Off   A E F   010990   43   18   13

        13 n x   m f g y 41 o b nogent june 18 1918

C. O. U. S. Troops Bourbonne les Bs.

        A 316   G G DIRECTS SECOND LIEUT H L HUNT V R C PROCEED TO

CHATILLION SUR SEINE REPORTING TO C O SECOND CORPS SCHOOL FOR DUTY

PERIOD TRAVEL DIRECTED NECESSARY IN THE MILITARY SERVICE

                                        PERKINS   1113A

        A TRUE COPY

        G. P. Thayer

        Captain, 3rd Cavalry,
             Adjutant.

HEADQUARTERS REMOUNT DEPOT.
ADVANCE SECTION, SERVICES OF SUPPLY.
AMERICAN EXPEDITIONARY FORCES.

France, 19 June '18.

SPECIAL ORDERS)
NO.   129)

E X T R A C T.

1.   In compliance with telegraphic instructions from Headquarters Advance Section, S.O.S., dated June 18, 1918, 2nd Lieutenant Harry F. Hunt, V.R.C., will proceed to Chatillion-sur-Seine, reporting upon arrival thereat to the Commanding Officer, 2nd Corps School for duty.

The travel directed is necessary in the military service.

x   x   x

By order of MAJOR SPRING:

A. P. THAYER.

Captain, 3rd Cavalry,
Adjutant.

APT/OES

Somewhere in France
June 23, 1918
My dear Mamma and Nellie,

And I am in another town tonight, just about 100 miles from where I was when I wrote you last week. Came here Friday and was enroute from about nine-thirty in the morning until almost nine at night but put in most of the time lying around waiting for trains as I had to change twice and wait each time.

I am still in what is called the advance section so can't tell you the name of the town or very much else. This is a town of about nine thousand people and is a typical old French town with its narrow crooked streets and old-fashioned houses.

There is an old church right next to this house that I heard was built in the fifth century and it looks it, too. I have a very nice room in a very old house. The floor is made from eight-inch boards and there are large cracks in between the boards. The floor slopes from two walls to the center of the room, and as the boards have been waxed and polished until they are slick, a fellow has to watch his step to keep from falling, especially just after you step off of the rug.

I have one of these old-fashioned, heavy, massive wood beds and it is about three feet high but is a fine place to sleep.

The bed is covered with heavy draperies, as we so often see in pictures of old-fashioned beds. But I throw the draperies back as I don't like them.

An old lady about fifty years old and her maid, a woman about 40, live here alone I think, and they certainly try to please me. They were up a dozen times the first day wanting to know if there was anything they could do etc. or I guess that is what they wanted. They can't talk English and I don't understand their lingo very well. From general appearances they must be pretty well off and I think they are of the very best class.

There is a wall around the house and I have to carry the key to get in by and it sure is a heavy bunglesome affair. I roughly marked around it here on the page. How do you think you would like to carry it around?

Mamma, I wish you could see some of the sights that are to be seen here; they are very interesting. They are just the things we have read about all our lives but you know I can't tell you as you could see it.

My duties here so far are very light and I don't believe I will stay very long, but one never can tell. There is an American aviation camp here and you can see and hear them flying all the time. I was out to the field this morning and watched the planes light and fly off, speaking as of birds. I am going to try and get a chance to take a flight if I can because it looks very interesting.

No mail now for almost three weeks, but there is a big ball-up somewhere in the mail for over here. No one is getting any to speak of. From the newspaper reports I guess the Austrians are about whipped in the new offensive and I think it will have quite an effect on the Austrian nation. Just let the Americans keep on coming. The sooner we get an army here the sooner the war will end.

I look for the Germans to commence another offensive very soon but I do believe the end is in sight. I think this year or next spring the German power will be on the ebb.

I sent Nellie an apron yesterday and one like it to Gesina. I have been intending to send the aprons for some time but simply kept putting it off.

I am sending you a picture of myself and you can see how I dress, with the Sam Brown belt and overseas cap. This is all for tonight so good night and write soon.

Lovingly, Harry

OK Lieut. Harry F. Hunt Vet. R.C.

A.E.F.

France Somewhere
July I, 1918
Dear Mamma and Nellie,

Well, at last I received some mail from you and it was the first I had had since the 5th of June. Received four letters from you and several from Gussie and I was very thankful for them.

I am still located where I was when I last wrote to you, but can't say how long I will be here. Of course that is something you never know over here, but I should worry. I like this place very well and would just as soon be here as any other place I know.

There is a school for "doughboy" infantry here and also the flying school. Met a KSAC graduate here the other day, a Lieut. Mudge, class of 1914, and several Wichita fellows. I am told that the Kansas National Guard was here some time ago for instruction.

A couple of officers were killed here Sat. when something got wrong with their aeroplane and it fell. They were only up about two hundred feet, but that is where it is dangerous. When they get higher, several thousand feet, they can usually right the plane.

I took about a 30-mile auto ride yesterday testing some horses for glanders down at some engineering camp and part of the time we were in a forest reserve. Saw one deer at a distance and several wild hogs. The hogs are comical-looking fellows, look a good deal like the true Arkansas hog, only a little bit worse. The country was very pretty and the roads were fine.

I am glad Nellie liked her collars even if they were old style, they cost thirty-two francs, that is, sixteen francs apiece. Sent Sis an apron the other day. How does the dear girl enjoy feeding the hungry people?

I think I have told you about all I do, just Vet. work in general and I am getting a good deal of good experience.

Now and then I go to a picture show or some kind of entertainment given by the Y.M. but not very often as they don't have anything very often here or where I was.

I don't know how table linen is here but will look around and will try to bring you some when I return. I don't think the submarines are getting the mail. It is just the way it is handled over here. I think we hear about all the large vessels that are sunk and I think the sub is almost afraid to attack the ships with a convoy.

I am glad to hear that U.S. is calling the men out because the sooner we get an army over here the sooner the war will be over and that is what we all want. The Italians hit Austria a good blow last week and it will take her some time if ever she gets over it, and two or three such blows handed to the Bosch will take about all the pep out of them. I guess from what I hear the American soldier is making Mr. Bosch sit up and take notice and that will take a good deal of the pep out of Mr. Bosch, too.

That was a very good letter from Frank P. but I knew there was some mistake as Frank is certainly a fine fellow. Would sure like to see his brother or Dr. Newton, his brother-in-law. I wrote him and Faith a letter the other day but did not mention anything about the note. I imagine the one he sent me will turn up some day, but you just keep that one.

We are having fine weather here now, the days are very warm and the nights cool so you see I can enjoy sleeping. We used to hear what we thought were the guns from the Front before I came here and they say you can hear them plain here early in the morning, but I am not up very early.

And so Sis has a liberty bond. That's good and when my eight come have them changed for the later issue so they will draw the higher rate of interest, but wish you would leave them in my name.

It took a good long time for the insurance policy to reach you but I guess they are kept very busy in Washington, D.C. Also glad to hear you are getting along so well, may the good work keep up and you will get the commutation of quarters by the time the Bill passes. It reads like this, that when an officer keeps up a home or dwelling besides his own self, he can draw the money and I think I should have it, don't you? So act accordingly. I could draw it over here but I will send it to you or have it sent.

I am sending you another request. I wish you would send me an Ingersol wrist-watch. The one I had went dead and these French watches are N.G. Just get a cheap one with a phosphorescent dial and the cigars just keep because they would be so dry when I did get them. Send the package 1st class and register it and I think it will come through better. I have not received the papers as yet. This is all I think of now so will close so write soon.

Lovingly, Harry
OK Lieut. Harry F. Hunt, Vet. R.C.
Amer. Exp. Forces France
A.P.O. 730

France Somewhere
July 7, 1918
Dear Mamma and Nellie,

Sunday evening and it has been one beautiful day, just a regular summer day, and we have had nice weather here for some time, the days are warm but the nights are cool.

The Fourth has come and passed and it was quite a day over here, too. The streets and houses were all decorated for the occasion. As you know the French declared it a fete day (holiday) and everybody celebrated. There was a big parade here in the morning and the parade was composed of Amer. soldiers, British soldiers, and French soldiers (the Amex, Tommies and Poilu,) and townspeople. The decorations were principally French flags and colors (blue, white and red) as there are very few Amer. flags here.

There was a ball game in the morning and a ball game and a track meet in the afternoon. The French people sure flocked out to all the games and the track meet and it seemed to amuse them very much. It was the first time they had ever seen anything of the kind and to watch the crowd was more amusing and entertaining to me than either the track meet or the ball game. The French people were always getting in the way, they did not know enough to keep off of the diamond or track or where to stay.

In Paree (Paris) I guess they celebrated right. I believe the Fourth was celebrated about everywhere this year but in Germany and they will know the effect of said celebration some of these days.

I have had several calls here to treat some horses for the French people and so far I have had very good success. One place I was they took me in and gave me some of the best (champagne) or I mean white wine that I have had since being in France, and it was better than the average champagne you buy at the Cafe.

Also ate dinner (evening meal) the Fourth with a French couple at their home and we sure had a fine meal. A cavalry officer here is billeted at their home and I was with him that p.m. and nothing would do but we stay there for supper. I certainly enjoyed the meal. The man is about fifty years old and his wife about forty-two and she is certainly une bonne cuisinier.

I guess they were giving the Germans a good entertainment up at the Front yesterday because we could hear the guns roaring very plain here. But that is what the Bosch needs. You know those big shells dropping about him take just a little bit of the pep out of him, and that is what he needs.

The American soldier is certainly proving to the world his ability to fight. I think the Bosch will change their minds soon about the Amex soldier, because he is making them sit up and take notice all the time. I see by tonight's paper where we lost another vessel, homeward bound. I wonder if it carried the mail and the package I sent Sis. Hope not. No mail from you this week, but I guess once every three weeks is as often as I need to look for it.

I heard a good one the other day and it was new so will tell it to you. It is reported that there is a move on foot in the United States to send Mr. Henry Ford to France as Chief Chaplain of the A.E.F. because he, with his tin lizzies, has been the cause of more H—I being shaken out of Americans in the last few years than anyone else. Wonder if it will work. Ha Ha.

This is all I think of now so will close and go to bed so good night and sweet dreams. Write soon.

Lovingly, Harry

MONTHLY SICK REPORT
for
SECOND CORPS SCHOOLS
A.P.O. No. 730

June 22 to June 30, 1918.

Total number of animals in organization:

Horses   84
Mules   3

- -

Horses:

1 Bruised Sole
7 Collar Galls
1 Fistula Withers
1 Injury

Mules:

3 Collar Galls

- -

Horses:

7 Mange (all exposed)

84 horses Malleined, all negative reactions, belonging to Co. E,
10th Engrs.

2nd Lt., V.R.C.

veterinarian

POSTES ET TÉLÉGRAPHES.

TÉLÉGRAMME.

(Voir au verso : FORMULE D'APPEL TÉLÉPHONIQUE.)

TAXE PRINCIPALE ....
TAXES ACCESSOIRES ....
TOTAL ....

NATURE DU TÉLÉGRAMME.	NUMÉRO.	NOMBRE DE MOTS.	HEURE DE DÉPÔT.	MENTIONS DE SERVICE (VOIES, ETC...) À TRANSMETTRE À LA FIN DU PRÉAMBULE.

Cadre réservé au service.

From

To L.C.O. Renault, Section A.E.F. French,

American arrived in French hospital [illegible]
Banville [illegible] to lack of food. Trouble arranging
English [illegible] feel certain [illegible]
[illegible]

Henry Sylvia

INDICATIONS DE TRANSMISSION :

Nom et adresse de l'expéditeur : (Ces indications ne sont taxées et transmises que sur la demande expresse de l'expéditeur.)

Prière d'écrire très lisiblement le télégramme.

Mod. n° 698. — 1392-25. (Juillet 1914. — Jésus 626.)

POSTES ET TÉLÉGRAPHES.

TÉLÉGRAMME.

(Voir au verso : FORMULE D'APPEL TÉLÉPHONIQUE.)

NATURE du Télégramme.	NUMÉRO.	NOMBRE DE MOTS.	HEURE DE DÉPÔT.	MENTIONS DE SERVICE (VOIES, ETC...) À TRANSMETTRE À LA FIN DU PRÉAMBULE.

TAXE PRINCIPALE
TAXES ACCESSOIRES
TOTAL

Cadre réservé au service.

From 2nd Lieut Henry J Hunt VRC Anglus (Marne)
Ec Chief Veterinarian A E F Tours unreadable

Horses dying here due to lack of grain
French say impossible to get grain

2 Line Copy
N.Y.Ti.

Mod. n° 698. — 1392-25. (Juillet 1914. — Jésus 626.)

Prière d'écrire très lisiblement le télégramme.

Nom et adresse de l'expéditeur :

(Ces indications ne sont taxées et transmises que sur la demande expresse de l'expéditeur.)

Télégramme.

INDICATIONS DE RÉCEPTION.		
Taxe principale.....		
Réponse payée.....		
TOTAL.....		

NATURE DU TÉLÉGRAMME ET DESTINATION.	ORIGINE.	NUMÉRO.	NOMBRE DE MOTS.	DATE.	HEURE DE DÉPÔT.	MENTIONS DE SERVICE.
of J'ust	Paris 44	29308	17		18.43p	

C. O. Veterinarian Detachement Spul

advise receipt of forage to forty five

avenue montaigne Paris

Colonel Wiliams.

AVIS. — Dans les télégrammes imprimés en caractères romains par l'appareil télégraphique, le premier nombre qui figure après le nom du lieu d'origine est un numéro d'ordre, le second indique le nombre des mots taxés, les autres désignent la date et l'heure du dépôt. Dans le service intérieur et dans les relations avec certains pays étrangers, l'heure de dépôt est indiquée au moyen des chiffres de 0 à 24.

Nº 700. — Écu jaune 668. — Juillet 1916.

Télégramme.

	NUMÉRO.	NOMBRE DE MOTS.	DATE.	HEURE DE DÉPÔT.	MENTIONS DE SERVICE.
ORIGINE. Paris	44/18	22	19	11.5	

INDICATIONS DE RÉCEPTION.

Taxe principale ......

Réponse payée. ......

Total. ......

NATURE DU TÉLÉGRAMME ET DESTINATION.

C.O Veterinary hopital anglais Mans

One Car of oats and one car hay leaving
Sierres tonight for your animals

Lt Col. Williams

AVIS. — Dans les télégrammes imprimés en caractères romains par l'appareil télégraphique, le premier nombre qui figure après le nom du lieu d'origine est un numéro d'ordre, le second indique le nombre des mots taxés, les autres désignent la date et l'heure du dépôt. Dans le service intérieur et dans les relations avec certains pays étrangers, l'heure de dépôt est indiquée au moyen des chiffres de 0 à 24.

N° 700. — Bon jaune 668. — Juillet 1916.

Télégramme.

INDICATIONS DE RÉCEPTION.		INDICATIONS DE TRANSMISSION. —

Taxe principale......

Réponse payée......

Total......

NATURE DU TÉLÉGRAMME ET DESTINATION.	ORIGINE.	NUMÉRO.	NOMBRE DE MOTS.	DATE.	HEURE DE DÉPÔT.	MENTIONS DE SERVICE.
of d'pol	Noisy le Sec no 44	92	41	21	46.10	

Aveyure Marne

Cois Veterinary détachement Gare French Veterinary hospital

Number mtmo fire seven seven period Car film
14276 containing oats 32000 pounds shipped today
Grema hay not available and will be shipped august
twenty second period

Dayro

AVIS. — Dans les télégrammes imprimés en caractères romains par l'appareil télégraphique, le premier nombre qui figure après le nom du lieu d'origine est un numéro d'ordre, le second indique le nombre des mots taxés, les autres désignent la date et l'heure du dépôt. Dans le service intérieur et dans les relations avec certains pays étrangers, l'heure de dépôt est indiquée au moyen des chiffres de 0 à 24.

N° 700. — Bon Jaune 668. — Juillet 1916.

Taxe principale ....
Réponse payée ....
TOTAL ....

INDICATIONS DE RÉCEPTION.

INDICATIONS DE TRANSMISSION.

ORIGINE. NUMÉRO. NOMBRE DE MOTS. DATE. HEURE DE DÉPÔT. MENTIONS DE SERVICE.

NATURE DU TÉLÉGRAMME ET DESTINATION.

C. O. Renouf Remain   Tonya
The detail twenty four hour from the
308 men Brigade now here lieutenant in charge
who has ordered return to (large) sundry anomas
animals thereunto

Name Effy
Egypt

Henry Hunt
Egypt VI

AVIS. — Dans les télégrammes imprimés en caractères romains par l'appareil télégraphique, le premier nombre qui figure après le nom du lieu d'origine est un numéro d'ordre, le second indique le nombre des mots taxés, les autres désignent la date et l'heure du dépôt. Dans le service intérieur et dans les relations avec certains pays étrangers, l'heure du dépôt est indiquée au moyen des chiffres de 0 à 24.

WEEKLY SICK REPORT
for
A.P.O. 730,
Second Corps Schools

For the week ending July 5, 1918.

To The Chief Veterinarian, A.E.F.

Carried forward from last report:

      Horses:
          1 bruised sole   *n - 1 3*
          6 collar galls   *n - 36*
          1 fistula withers *n 41*
          1 injury   *R 18*

      Mules:
          2 collar galls   *n - 36*

      Horses:
          7 mange (all exposed) *2 10*

New cases:

      Horses:
          2 sprained tendeons *n 6 9*

Treatment of mange has been commenced.

Total number of animals in organization:

      84 horses
      3 mules

                                   2nd Lt., V.R.C.

This letter was written him by a friend, Pauline Montgomery, from Wichita, Kansas. It was on The Union Stock Yards National Bank letterhead and dated July 15, 1918. The postage on the envelope, sent from Wichita to France, was two cents.

Dear Doc:

I got your card Saturday and was certainly glad to hear from you. That was my first message from overseas.

Gussie, of course, has kept me as well informed as she could regarding you, but I don't get to see her very often.

Marie is now in Seattle with Joe, and Glenn is in camp about six miles out of Seattle. Haven't heard from Marie since she got there, but think I will soon.

I suppose Gussie has told you before this that I went and "jumped the broomstick". I was married June 19 to Elmer Montgomery, who is now in Camp Lee, Virginia, ready to sail at any time. He is in the Veterinary Corps, so you ought to be congenial friends. If you ever run across each other, I hope you will become friends.

Of course it is awfully hard to have to be separated before we had been married long enough to even quarrel, but on the other hand I'm proud to be a soldier's wife, and am mighty glad he isn't a slacker. He enlisted April 7, was in Jefferson Barracks for a couple weeks and then was sent to Ft. Riley. He was sent to Camp Lee right after the first of this month. It's some experience to be married and a "widow" all within a week. I kinda (some word isn't it) wish you and Gussie had married before you left. Maybe you do, too. I don't think she would think any more of you, for if I read the signs right, she's all yours anyway. But don't worry, you'll soon be back, and will enjoy your freedom and happiness all the more for having suffered hardships. I'm some preacher, don't you think? Anyway I'm happy and want everyone else to be.

Wishing you luck and prosperity, and hoping for a sudden termination of the war. I am as ever,

Your sincere friend,

Pauline

France Somewhere in France
July 15, 1918
Dear Mamma and Nellie,

This is a very pretty day here, it is nice and cool and very enjoyable out. Yesterday and night before last it rained just a little but not enough to do much good.

Yesterday was the French Independence Day but it passed very quiet here, not near the excitement there was on the Fourth and while it was a holiday for all U.S. troops there was very little excitement here. I guess in Paree (Paris) and the larger towns there was quite a little excitement. I have been kept fairly busy since last writing. I have very little to do and I guess I am getting lazy, but it doesn't seem like I have very much time for anything either.

Will have a picture to send you pretty soon, about the only good one I got out of my first six that I can send you. Your letter No. 5 mailed June 14 received yesterday, the first letter in over two weeks from you. My mail is certainly balled up it seems and there are so many the same way over here.

I was glad to know that everything was allright and that Nellie thinks she will finish this summer. She should try to get a position somewhere that pays so much a month and you are better off in the end. She must have plenty of nerve and spunk and not be afraid to try things. You know none of us is perfect but it takes plenty of nerve and spunk to get along.

Don't know much more now than I did when I wrote before, only I guess from what I hear and see there are large numbers of American soldiers coming abroad this summer. The division Ray O. was with at Camp Travis is located just south of here, but I don't think he came with them from what I hear. Would sure like to see the boy just for a good chat.

How does Nellie's man like the Army and what does he think of Camp Pike? It is sure one lonesome camp but not half as bad as it is over here in sunny France. Too bad Jennie thinks the way she does about her boy. She ought to be proud to have a boy who could go. If we don't whip those Bosch now, we will have to hoe cabbage the rest of our lives to keep them in sauerkraut, and I never did like to hoe very well. You know?

Sis has the right way of thinking about the big husky and everyone should think the same way. You bet, Mother, I am glad I did as I did and always will be glad I did just that way, and some day I think all the boys in khaki will be glad they were called.

The American troops here that I have seen are sure in fine spirits and they all seem anxious to get a chance at the Kaiser. I think the Bosch is commencing to realize that the "handwriting is on the wall," and I think that as soon as the Allies open up on him right good and proper, that it will take about two-thirds of his pep away. And I kinda think the Allies will start a drive this fall and a few things I know but can't write to you will help the Bosch keep their eyes open.

When we (the U.S.) get our artillery and aeroplanes over here in force something is going to have to pop, and I think they will soon be here. I am sure glad to know the wheat is so good. That means plenty of bread for the Allies.

Sure glad to know the Rock Island got enough pep to fix their depot; it needed it bad enough. Just wish I could see it, but not until the war is over, then they can't take me home quick enough.

Save about a gallon of those cherries for me. I will be hungry as usual when I get there. Wish Nellie would send me a couple of those pictures of Gussie and me, the one that I have my hat on. I want them for a reason. I know she will enjoy presenting them for her dear brother. This is all for this time so I will ring off so bye-bye and write soon.

Harry

A prolific letter writer, Lt. Hunt kept up a correspondence with many friends and relatives. He received this letter from another friend, Marie Ayer Van Horn.

Seattle, Wash. July 19, 1918
Lieut. Harry F. Hunt, V.R.C., A.E.F.,
Somewhere in France
Dear Harry:

Your interesting letter of June 2nd was received just before leaving for Seattle, and as we have been pretty busy since arriving I have delayed answering it. We were certainly mighty glad to hear from you and to know that you are getting along so nicely.

Left Wichita on July 1st and arrived in Seattle the night of the 4th, and I don't have to tell you that there were two very happy people, for I am sure you know. Joe had been out here just ten weeks. He had a very nice little five-room modern house rented and we had a place to go to right away as he had rented it furnished.

He is still working in the yards, but I am very much afraid if they keep on taking men that they will take him before long. However, I am not worrying much and will just make the best of it like others have to.

I suppose Gussie has written you about Pauline marrying the soldier boy. It was certainly some great surprise to everyone.

I was up and stayed all night with Gussie before I came out here and she was down at the station when I came. Believe me, Doc, you have got some brave little girl in Wichita.

You will also be somewhat surprised to know that *Glenn J.* is out here at *Ft. Lawton.* We went out to see him last *Sunday* and he was surely glad to see us. He is coming in for supper with us tomorrow night. I asked him what he would like for me to fix for him and he said, "I don't care just so you have biscuits," so I guess it will have to be biscuits. Wish you could be here with us, too. There are quite a few *Wichita* fellows out here, but we only know one or two more.

We sure do enjoy your letters. *Joe* has been intending to write, but when he was out here before I came, he couldn't get very many written more than mine, but he will write you before long. He has to go to work about 6:15 a.m. and it is after 5:10 when he gets home, so you see he is kept pretty busy.

Write to us just whenever you can, and I'll try and answer sooner next time.

With all best wishes, I am,
Sincerely,
Marie Ayer Van Horn

Somewhere in France
Aug . 2, 1918
My dear Mamma and Nellie,

Your good letter of June 26 was received today and I will proceed at once to answer it as I have nothing else to do today. About all of the horses have been transferred away from this station and it leaves me with very little to do but I don't think I will be here long. I have put in for a transfer and expect to hear from it any time.

It has been trying to rain again today but has succeeded only in drizzling, but that is about the only kind of rain we have in France. I have only seen it really rain a few times since I have been here...

You received the insurance policy did you not—seems to me like you mentioned it in one of your letters not long ago...

And so my little sister is working at the Botany Department. Hope the dear girl gets along all right but tell her to try and keep away from the hour work, and get a steady job in something in her line. She should get more money than that. Don't be afraid. You know it takes nerve to get along in this world.

Sorry to hear your garden is drying up so bad and here is hoping you get some rain or have it before now... I collected the commutation of quarters money here today and will send it to you. It amounts to something like $29.00 a month, but I will draw it here and send it to you by money order, because it takes a lot of red tape and trouble to send it through the government. So from April 16, 1918, as long as I am in the Army they will allow me commutation of quarters...

Believe me I am saving all I can. I will need it when I return to the good old U.S.A. and there is very little to spend it on over here that interests me, although I am going to have to buy some clothes this winter. You know they will wear out and they cost like everything over here, but not so high when you take everything into consideration. They are no higher here than they are in the States.

I will write concerning the liberty bonds, but I think I told them to send them to you. I received a letter the other day from Lester Stryker. He is with the Kansas troops... I also met Lieut. Standley here today who finished KSAC in 1912. I knew him well there but hardly recognized him here, he had taken on so much weight. He told me where several of the fellows are that I used to know. He is an engineer...

I suppose the papers are full of the present fight or battle and the way the American soldiers are fighting. Guess the Bosch will change his mind about our men's fighting qualities. They are holding their own with the best of the Allied troops and are teaching the best German regiments a thing or two, but that has always been the way with our men and they never have failed yet.

Did you receive the money order I sent June 1st to you, or about that time for $100.00. Yes, I received the letter you sent me from Frank P. O, Yes, if you have any magazines you don't want just send them to me if they will allow you. Send them by mail and the cheapest way. I won't get over half of them anyhow. This is all I think of so will close so let me hear from you soon.

Lovingly, Harry

France Somewhere
Aug. 11, 1918
Dear Mamma and Nellie,

This is a very cool evening I can tell you, and if it keeps this weather up long I will have to get something to burn, and fuel is mighty scarce over here... It has rained here every day for the past week. I guess the rainy season has commenced once more. Wish you had some of this rain, or has it rained where you are? Does me lots of good to ask questions like that as it will be Christmas before I receive an answer to this letter, no doubt.

What can I send you for Christmas this year? Wish I was coming to eat dinner with you that day, but by Xmas 1919 I hope I can be with you again and from the way things look now I think I will.

I shipped part of the horses away from here yesterday and will ship the rest just as soon as they get in condition, and then I go, but I know not where. That song, "Where Do We Go From Here", comes home quite often over here.

I have changed rooming houses here in town. I like my new room much better because it is much neater and cleaner and here I have a wood floor and before it was a stone floor.

I have some postcards I bought in Paris that I will send you some of these days if I don't forget it. Have not as yet received the package with the watch and ring, but trust I will soon. I don't think I will send home for anything else. It takes so long for it to arrive here, so anything I need I will buy over here.

I have been taking daily horseback rides of about ten kilometers and I enjoy them very much. I have a fine horse here to ride, but he is just getting in condition good and I will soon have to send him away, but such is life over here.

I am sending you a copy of the claim for commutation of quarters bill as I fill out here, so read it over and you know what the bill is. This is not much of a letter but it is all I think of now so will close, so write soon.

Lovingly, Harry

Lt. Hunt's last diary entry, dated August 12:
Arrived in Anglure Marne with the French at a Vet Hospital. I am stationed at St. Just.

From "Final Report of Gen. John J. Pershing, Commander-In-Chief, American Expeditionary Forces," Washington Government Printing Office, 1920. Page 94:
"The Stars and Stripes was a weekly newspaper conceived with the idea of increasing the morale of American troops by providing a common means of voicing the thought of the entire American Expeditionary Forces. Edited and managed by enlisted men who declined promotion, preferring to remain in the ranks in order better to interpret the spirit of the Army, it was a great unifying force and materially aided in the development of an esprit de corps. It lent loyal and enthusiastic support to Army athletics and to the educational program. In leading the men of our Army to laugh at their hardships, it was a distinct force for good and helped to create a healthy viewpoint. The campaign it conducted for the benefit of French orphans resulted in a fund of 2,250,000 francs."

France Somewhere
Aug . 13, 1918
My dear Mother and Nellie,

Just arrived here yesterday and I was sure one tired human. I only slept about three hours the night before and was on the go most of the time. However, I slept very good last night and feel pretty good today.

Now I am at a French Vet. hospital and there are plenty of wounded horses here, part of them American. I am here to look after them.

This is a very small town and I am a good ways north of where I was when I last wrote. There is only one other American officer here and we eat with the French officers and have a very good mess. My room here is the poorest I have had since being in France but you can expect that in little towns.

As long as I am here I will get my mail through the French post office and I guess I will be lucky if I ever get any mail now. Received a letter from Gussie just before coming here, the first one in three weeks. It has been a long time since I have heard from you.

We sure are getting good news from the Front. The French say that never since the war started has the news been so good, and with the arrival of so many American soldiers they sure are feeling good and I guess the Bosch is getting one good setback. Wonder what he will say was the cause of this defeat, but it will be according to his plans I guess, but I think this is the turning point of the war and from now on the Hun will continue to go back.

From reports the Bosch is sure respecting the fighting qualities of the American soldier and he will learn more about our men, much to his sorrow, as time passes.

I subscribed for the "Stars and Stripes," a paper printed by the Amer. E.F. over here for you and you should commence to receive it before you get this letter. If you don't, let me know.

The weather has been fine the last three days, hot days and cool nights. Will close for this time and write more later. Will mail this in the French P.O. so I imagine it will take a long time for you to receive it. So bye-bye and write soon.

Harry

France Somewhere
Aug. 20, 1918
Dear Mamma and Nellie,

This is a cool cloudy day and acts very much like it will rain, but I doubt if it succeeds. Now that a good rain would be welcomed it won't come.

Everything is going along just as good as could be expected here, and I have plenty of work, but the facilities are not very good, but you know in war times we can't always have what we want. This is the most lonesome town I have been in since arriving in France and as it is a very small burg the accommodations are far from being what I am used to.

We can hear the roar of the cannons all times of the day and night and the people here claim that during the big battle of the Marne (the second one) the tables rocked so it was hard to keep the dishes on them, but I sometimes doubt that. There were three Bosch planes flying around here the other evening, the French people claimed, and believe me there were no lights aglow in this burg. But as far as I know the Bosch dropped no bombs close. But they bomb a nearby town quite often I hear. That was a cowardly trick the Bosch tried on the American seaports towns the other day and I am glad it failed, but it shows the true nature of the barbarous Hun. I am beginning to think that the only way to cure him is to give him a dose of his own medicine and I think the time is coming soon when K. Bill will have wished he had not been quite so generous with his "Kultur" as he calls it. I think these last two pokes the Allies have given the Hun will help to take just a little of his pep away and when the Amer. get here in force something is going to happen. So the sooner they come, the sooner the war will be over, and the sooner the war is over and the Bosch is whipped the sooner this old world will be a safe place for people to live.

I have received no mail since arriving here and chances are I won't very soon. The country here is very flat and from the looks of the soil it is not very good. I have been in swimming here several times and I enjoy it very much, and it is the only way we have of taking a bath as I don't think there is a bathtub in town. I will close for this time so let me hear from you soon. Oh, yes, $105.00 of that last M.O. is for you. So bye-bye.

Lovingly, Harry

This letter, written by his mother to Harry on August 25, 1918, refers to Nellie's friend, Merle W. Converse, whom she later married.

No. 16.
Manhattan, Kansas,
August 25, 1918.

My dear Harry—Your very welcome letters of July 23rd and Aug. 3rd came to us Aug. 20th, also the money orders, for which I thank you. I put $100 in the bank for you, and will use the balance.

We have sent your box with the articles you requested, and hope you get them. Also mailed you two magazines. They told us at the post office just to tie a stout string around them, not to stick the wrapper on. There are continued stories in these, and we will send you the October numbers so you can get them all. It is hard to get a magazine without a continued story.

We got the other $100.00 the last of June. Haven't heard anything of your liberty bonds.

Was much pleased with the picture. You certainly are looking well, and it looks odd to see the oxen and cart. We received the insurance policy and wrote you when it came. Mrs. Lizzie Wood was here the other afternoon and stayed for supper. She is the twins' mother. They were taken in this last draft, and sent someplace in Georgia.

We are glad you get a letter from home occasionally. It seems we write so many, but we are told not to send papers but to send clippings in letters as they are more apt to go, so many papers never go. But we can easily understand there must be scads of mail, both letters and papers, and of course some is bound to go astray, but we write and send something each week, so be hopeful.

We heard Milburn Stryker was sent to Camp Funston, but have not seen him. Laura Schell came to see Robert. He was at the hospital here, had throat trouble, so had his tonsils removed. Was at the College taking voice culture.

We had a good rain Thursday evening, about two inches, the papers say, and we are more comfortable since. While the sun is hot, the air is cool and fresh. Mr. Raburns who live on the west have been gone to Ann Arbor, Mich. a year. They came home today, and I said how nice and cool it is. They said, "Oh! do you think so, why where we were, we had to have a fire in July to keep warm." It hardly seems possible.

I bought a new pair of slippers, and will get a dress and other things, thanks to the government money, which I am so thankful for. So many have asked if I did not get something from the government, and now I can tell them when they ask.

Nellie mailed you a letter Wednesday. Her friend spent Wednesday here and stayed until Thursday. He is a 2nd Lieut. and will be an instructor at Camp Taylor for awhile. Donald McLeod got 2nd Lt. We knew none of the others. Was at Sunday School today. Am sending some pieces (clippings). Reed Crooks is from Fredonia. He writes about Allen Frater and Clifford Byerly.

We are saving the cherries until you help lick the Kaiser. Lots of love from Mother.

We are saving the cherries until you help lick the Kaiser.

France Somewhere
Aug . 26, 1918
Dear Mamma and Nellie,

It has been real cloudy today and nice and cool, for which I am thankful. I am kept pretty busy here with one thing and another. It seems like there is no end to the work turning up, but you know it makes time pass more rapidly.

Received your two letters written on July 3 and July 10 last week and contents were sure read with pleasure. I am glad to hear everything is going good. It seems kinda queer to read your letters about the Fourth of July when the Fourth has passed so long, I have almost forgotten what I did.

I wish I could come and eat some of your roasting ears. They sound like they would taste good. I have not seen a stalk of corn since coming to France. I don't think they raise very much, if any, here.

Tell Ray next time you see him I rode all one afternoon in a car trying to locate him in the 90th Div. when I was near it over here, before I found out he stayed on that side. That was sure some feat of Donald Hudson. Yes, I remember him and remember of reading the report in the paper here but little did I think it was he.

And now I am going to try and answer my little sister's question, but will say I believe she is able to ask more questions now than ever where I am. Now I am with the French Army in a Vet. Hosp. and there is one other American officer here and 24 men. Other places I have been there has always been many Americans and in regard to whether I can parley Francais, if you would hear me sometimes trying to, you would not think so. I sure have a job trying to talk it sometimes with a dictionary. However, with plenty of time and patience I can tell them, as a rule, what I want.

Paris is west of me now and I have visited it once but had not when I received your letter. Was up there Sunday and Monday on a business (?) trip and believe me it is some town, and I sure enjoyed my visit there but did not get to stay long enough to see much of the town. But I was sure tired when I arrived here last night and I saw a good many interesting sights while there but can't tell you as I cannot remember the names but I have just this to say: Paris is sure one grand town and I don't blame the French a bit for not wanting the Bosch to capture it.

Will mention a few of the things I saw that I remember, Eiffel Tower, Napoleon's Tomb, the Ferris wheel, that big Bosch cannon etc. etc. I have a few postcard views I will send you, as you know Paris is the only town in France we can send cards from. One would never know by being in Paris that there was a war going on. Everything is on the move and everything moves. I sure saw some fine sculpture work there. The buildings are only six stories high but they are certainly pretty, so much carved stone, etc.

In regards to news, wish you would tell me some. I only see an Amer. newspaper about every five days and the news I get out of the French paper I just guess about.

Don't worry, the war will end sometime but I don't think I can eat this Christmas dinner with you. But I think this winter we'll whip the Bosch and then next spring the war will end, because he (the Bosch) is certainly getting it right and left now and I don't think the Bosch can stand heavy losses this late in the game. I think the handwriting is on the wall for the Kaiser.

Don't think Sis is so anxious for her brother to get his feet under his mother's table as she is somebody else's brother???

Gussie told me in one of her letters a good while ago she was going to or had written you a letter that night. I only receive about one out of every ten of her letters. How does Sis' friend like the Army?

I sent you, or rather had the "Stars and Stripes" sent to you, in July so please let me know if you received it or not. Also if you get the money, $255.00 I sent to you several weeks ago, $105.00 of the amount is what the commutation of quarters pays to you, or to me for you.

I can hear the hum of the cute little mosquito very plain as I sit here in the candle glow and write this. Now and then they get sociable and bite. More mosquitoes here than I have seen or heard anywhere in France. Will close and write to Gussie so good night and sweet dreams and write soon.

Lovingly, Harry

No. 17
Manhattan, Kansas
Sept. 2, 1918
Monday eve.
My dear boy-

No letter from you for two weeks, but we are expecting two tomorrow. Do you think we will get them? We had a good shower last evening and it is nice and cool this eve. We mowed the yard, and we had a two in. rain two weeks ago, so the crabgrass ought to grow if there is not much bluegrass left. We noticed several bunches of bluegrass. I think the crabgrass is pretty if it's kept cut short. We sowed turnip and radish seed, but are not very hopeful of them getting big as saucers...

Nellie had a card from Jesse Corsart. He is at Houston, Texas, taking lessons in night flying. These flying machines seem to be getting quite common. I see by the paper this evening one passed over Manhattan today going from Topeka to Camp Funston and two made the flight one day last week, but we did not get to see either. Did not know anything about them going until after it was all over....

This is Labor Day, first Monday in Sept. We washed, cleaned the hen house, and wiped up the kitchen and dining room floors. Now since this rain it will not get so dusty. I see in this eve paper there is a car of Alberta peaches on the track, at $3.50 per bushel, that is pretty high but then everything is so high. We have plenty of potatoes yet, and we have been getting from two to five eggs a day-they are 43 cents, but 48 cents at the college. Corn is $2.00 a bushel, oats 90 cents so you know it costs something to feed the chickens. We haven't had a fry yet but will in a few days.

Lots of changes on this street. The Veterinary Fraternity is going to be in the house the Sigma Nu's had, and Mr. Chapin has sold his place, and the Chi Omega, a sorority, has rented it...

I fixed up our liberty bonds some time ago, the first interest is due Sept. 15 but haven't received yours yet.

I did not go to church or Sunday school yesterday, had such a splitting headache, but Nellie went to Sunday school-you know she has charge of the little folks. Marie and her mother were here last week and we went out south of town and got some fine melons-three big fellows for 50 cents. We have had such good melons this year...

Nellie will write in a few days and send the "funny sheet." It's pretty good this time. Be good. Lots of love from home.

Lovingly, Mother

France Somewhere
September 6, 1918
Dear Mamma and Nellie,

I have been just a little bit slow this week in writing to you but I have had quite a good deal a-doing as you will see. Monday night or rather Monday noon things so happened that it was deemed advisable for me to go to Paris and as it did not take much persuasion I went and spent that night and the next day and night and part of the next day. While I was very busy a good part of the time while there, I certainly had a good time also. Paris is certainly one good town, and I like it very much.

While there I met Lieut. M.S. Agnew, Aggie football captain 1915, and a very good pal of mine while in school. I certainly enjoyed being with him. Went to a couple of shows and they were shows too, and I enjoyed seeing them. While everything about it was in the French language and I did not understand very much of it, I enjoyed the shows and especially the music, which was great.

Believe me, Paris is some good old town and little does one realize while there that a great battle is raging as close as it is. But such is the life of the Parisian. While there I bought a new suit or rather enough serge to get one made, bought the goods from the Amer. Commissary and got it very cheap I thought, considering everything. Don't know when I can get it made up as there are no tailors here, but don't think I will be in this town more than three weeks longer from present dope.

I heard this evening that the Hun aeroplanes raided a little town about ten miles from here today, but don't think they did any damage.

This has sure been my lucky week in getting mail. I have received four letters from you, four from Gussie, and one from the serum plant and believe me every one of them was welcomed. More mail than I have received any one week since I have been over here, so you see that is a very good record and makes a fellow think that perhaps he will get some more soon.

Nellie should have her apron by now because Gussie has received hers. Wish the watch would hurry and arrive as the one I have doesn't run very good. Thanks for the pictures.

We have been having very nice weather here lately and the nights are always nice and cool, so one can always enjoy sleeping very much.

The horses I have here are commencing to look much better and I hope soon to have them well and back in action. Will send the best away in a few days. I have been having some very good horseback rides lately and I certainly enjoy riding. For short distances there is nothing that beats it.

The ring I am wearing in the picture is a silver one I bought over here. Is that all right? (Sis take notice). I am glad to hear that Nellie is soon to get her diploma. How does she like being a college graduate? Guess she does not feel so big now does she. That is very nice that she is receiving so many presents but perhaps she will need them sometime.

The news is sure good these days from the Front and may it continue that way is my wish, but I don't think the Germans are as near whipped as the papers say they are, although I think they are commencing to realize that they are fighting a losing battle.

Tell Ray and Merle (Nellie's fiance) when they come over to bring plenty of heavy shoes and suits but bring all serge or whipcord suits as we cannot wear the O.D. woolen here, also a heavy raincoat, one with a detachable lining as the heavy over-coats are not much over here because it rains too much. I think they can buy clothing cheaper in the U.S. than here. But at the same time remember that it gets very hot here in summer.

This is all for tonight so will close so write soon.

Lovingly, Harry

Soilly 6:45 P.M.
80 Quai

8:45

Sixth Key

Signy
also

Sept 22/18

Telegramme

Tours -44/263/ 43   18.45

2 N.D. Lt Harry Hunt, V.C.

French Vet. Hospital Anglune

M. 195. Proceed to headquarters first
Army, Reporting upon arrival to Commanding
General for duty with assistant chief
Veterinarian first Army. Travel direct
is necessary in the military service

Gavanonos
A. C. S.

A True Copy
of telegram

Harry F. Hunt

2nd Lieut. V.C.

9 P.M
9/26/18
Bar Le Duc

WAR DEPARTMENT

(Bureau or Office.)

Voucher No.

MILEAGE VOUCHER

APPROPRIATION : _____ Symbol _____ $ _____

APPROPRIATION : _____ Symbol _____ $ _____

THE UNITED STATES TO *2nd Lieut. Harry F Hunt*, DR. *V.C. apo*
APO 743 ADDRESS: *110 Hdqrts & M.C. Amer E.F. 743*

From *Sept 22*, 191*8* to *Sept 28*, 1918, for
mileage from *Anglure (Marne)* to *Camp Perrin*
Transportation furnished between *St Dizier and Soully*
Tigny and Camp Perrin

I CERTIFY that the foregoing account is correct and that transportation, either in kind or on Government
Transportation Request, was not used except as stated above.

DO NOT SIGN IN DUPLICATE.

Harry F Hunt
2nd Lieut V.C.

This space for use of paying officer.

Object Symbol		Amount	U. S. Notations
	_____ miles at 7 cents _____		
	Actual expenses as per statement attached _____		
	Deductions at 3 cents per mile : _____ miles,		
	account transportation furnished _____		
	Amount to be paid _____		
			EXAMINED BY

Paid by check No. _____, dated _____, 191__, of _____
on _____, in favor of payee named above, for $ _____.

OR

Received _____ 191__, of _____
IN CASH, the sum of _____ dollars and _____ cents
in full payment of the above account.

$ ▇▇▇▇▇▇▇

REIMBURSEMENT. — Supplies, Services, and Transportation, Quartermaster Corps, 191__ _____ $ _____

Fortin et Cie, Nevers-Paris.

FRANCE, 1st October 1918.

From: 2nd Lieutenant Harry F. Hunt, V.C.

To: The Chief Surgeon, A. E. F.

Subject: Personal Report.

1.   On duty H.V.A. No. 1, French, September 1, 1918, to September 22, 1918, at Anglure (Marne).

2.   Enroute from Anglure (Marne) to 35th Division, September 23, 1918, to September 29, 1918, per Telegraphic Instructions, Hdqrs. S.O.S. dated September 22, 1918, and verbal instructions Army Veterinarian, 1st Army.

3.   On duty with 110th Headquarters Train & Military Police, September 30, 1918, per par. 2 S.O. No. 232, Hdqrs. 35th Division, dated September 28, 1918.

                              Harry F. Hunt.

TWENTY ONE GET DEGREES

GRADUATED FROM K. S. A. C. AT END OF SUMMER SCHOOL SESSION

Four in Military Service Granted Degrees in Absentia—Only Five Men in Class

Twenty one students, four of them in military service, received degrees at the close of the summer session of the college. The class consisted of young women and five young men.

The total enrolment in the summer session, exclusive of young men in the army taking courses, was 518, an increase of 37 over the enrolment in the summer of 1917. Besides these regular students, the college has given training in mechanical work, wireless telegraphy, and other subjects to 880 drafted men. This makes a total in residence this summer of 1,398.

This year there is likely to be almost no time—except on Sundays—when no persons are receiving instruction on the campus. The regular college work, including the summer session, is conducted for six days a week during 45 weeks of the year. The training of drafted men will fill at least part of the remainder.

Degrees were awarded as follows:

Bachelor of science in home economics—Estella May Albin, Grainfield; Florence Wiletta Baird of Cherryvale; Helen Crane, Kansas City, Mo.; Elsie May Griffin, Nickerson; Esther Gladys Hilbish, Lewis; Leona May Hoag, Ionia; Nellie Elizabeth Hunt, Manhattan; Mary Helen Hunter, Anthony; Mamie Adelaide Norlin, McCracken; Amanda Christine Olson, Brookville; Edna Irene Rawlings, Eureka; Maud Ernestine Sjolander, Topeka.

Bachelor of science in agriculture—Cecil Lyman McFadden, Stafford; Herbert Proudfit Miller, Kansas City, Kan. (in military service); Percy Le Roy Depue, Girard (in military service.)

Bachelor of science—Blanche May Berger, Sylvan Grove; Lulu Maude Berger, Sylvan Grove; Gladys Irene Garnard Rude, Wellington; Eva Emmaline Wood, Manhattan.

Bachelor of science in flour mill engineering—Paul Leroy Mann, Manhattan (in military service; Herbert John Helmkamp, Newton, (in military service.)

Dear Son

From the Stars and Stripes
(Sent to Mrs. A. M. Barthel, Topeka, by her son, Sgt. Herbert C. Barthel, from overseas.)

I wish I had the power to write
The thoughts wedged in my heart tonight
As I sit watching that small star—
And wondering how and where you are.

You know, Son, it's a funny thing
How close a war can always bring
A family, who for years with pride
Have kept emotion deep inside.

I'm sorry that when you were small
I let reserve build up the wall,
I told you real men never cried—
And it was Moms who always dried
Your tears and smoothed the hurt away
So that you soon went back to play.

Now suddenly I find my Son
A full-grown man with childhood done.
Tonight you're far across the sea
Waging war for men like me.

Well, somehow, pride and what is right
Just doesn't seem to go tonight.
I find my eyes won't stay quite dry;
I find that sometimes men do cry—
And if we stood here face to face
I'm 'fraid we'd find men do embrace.

Son, all Dads are a funny lot
And if I've failed you in some spot
It's not because I loved you less,
It's just this cussed manliness.

But if I had the power to write
The thoughts wedged in my heart tonight—
The words would ring out loud and true,
I'm proud, my boy, yes, proud of you!

—Author Unknown.

Please return—

From "Final Report of Gen. John J. Pershing, Commander-In Chief, American Expeditionary Forces, Washington Government Printing Office, 1920, pages 80-81:

"37. On July 20, 1917, a Provost Marshal General was appointed with station in Paris, and later the department was organized as an administrative service with the Provost Marshal General functioning under the First Section, General Staff. The department was developed into four main sections—the Military Police Corps which served with divisions, corps and armies and in the sections of the Services of Supply; the Prisoner of War Escort Companies; the Criminal Investigation Department; and the Circulation Department. It was not until 1918 that the last-mentioned department became well trained and efficient. On October 15, 1918, the strength of the Corps was increased to 1 per cent of the strength of the American Expeditionary Forces, and provost marshals for armies, corps, and dlvisions were provided.

"The military police of the American Expeditionary Forces developed into one of the most striking bodies of men in Europe. Wherever the American soldier went, there our military police were on duty. They controlled traffic in the battle zone, in all villages occupied by American troops, and in many cities through which our traffic flowed; they maintained order, so far as the American soldiers were concerned, throughout France and in portions of England, Italy, Belgium, and occupied Germany. Their smart appearance and military bearing and the intelligent manner in which they discharged their duties left an excellent impression of the typical American on all with whom they came in contact."

CHAPTER VI

ADVANCE TO THE BATTLEFRONT

France Somewhere
Sept. 27, 1918
Dear Mamma and Nellie,

Just a line tonight cause I am some tired boy. Have been on the go since Sunday and will not get to my destination until tomorrow. I think I am being assigned to the 35th Div. which is the Kansas and Missouri National Guard so guess I will meet quite a number of my old friends.

I saw Dr. Newton's brother the other day and was with him about two days. He is with the 35th Div. so may see him again soon. I am now very close to the Front and will go closer tomorrow. Passed over several of the old battlefields today and saw many of the ruins from some of the battles.

The only baggage I have now is my bedroll and grip as I had to leave my trunks behind. You can only carry 75 pounds with you. I have traveled in every kind of conveyance imaginable in coming to the Front. It is a very interesting sight to see up here, the way they move provisions etc. to the Front. I have seen very many trucks, more than I ever thought there were in the world. This is all for tonight as I am too tired to write more, so good night.

Lovingly, Harry
OK Lieut. Harry F. Hunt Vet Corp.
Am. E.F.
Unassigned

Annie's letter, which she had numbered at the top "No. 22nd", to her son, was written from Manhattan, Kansas, September 30, 1918.

My dear Harry-

Your very welcome letter of Aug. 6th is at hand, and we are glad to know you have had some of the letters written to you, and hope you are receiving the others by now. about the time they find out where you are, and where to send your mail you are sent some other place, and it takes time to locate you again.

I only hope you get that box and some of the magazines we have sent you. This is a cool evening, has been cold all day, at least I had to close all the windows the wind blew so hard.

We had a fried chicken of our own yesterday, and will use the roosters. Feed is so high, corn is $2.00 a bushel, eggs 48 cents per doz., 4 cents each. We got four yesterday and two today. Butter is 63 cents a lb.

The first paper of the "Stars and Stripes" came Friday, also a card from Ray Olinger saying he had arrived safely overseas, nothing more, so you may see him. We are glad for the paper and enjoy reading it.

Your four liberty bonds came today of $100 each (making $400.00). Is that as it should be? They draw 4 1/4 percent interest, that is what you wanted, is it not? They are the same as ours, and the first interest is due Nov. 15th, 1918.

We had a letter from Uncle Billy, you know he went to Portland, Oregon to work in the shipyards for the gov. He is not much pleased with the work, only worked two days, says that's enough for him. Says not to write until we hear from him again.

The town and scenery is lovely, the roses are almost as large as cabbages, think of that. He sent an envelope of postal views, beauties, and with the ones you sent of Paris we are well supplied.

You were fortunate to find that Mr. Agnew. Did you know he was stationed at Paris? Mrs. D. A. Dodd expects to go over to Paris sometime soon, her daughter Margaret is in Paris with an aunt. The aunt is very wealthy and influential so we hear.

Am glad the horses are improving, poor creatures. I guess they are in no hurry to get back into action.

The home folks (at Fredonia, Kansas) are well. Ralph stays in town and goes to school. I do not know who teaches at Grand Valley this winter. Myrt and family had been over to see them. We haven't heard from Eugene since the letter we sent to you. We wrote to Aunt Dollie and asked her to visit, hope *she can come.*

Next time you write just tell us the number of our letter you receive. I imagine you have about No. 13 telling about the things we sent. Am glad to hear of your new suit or material for one. That means that you will be warmly dressed. Everything in wearing apparel is very high here.

Nellie has a lot of clippings to send. She gets her big envelopes at the college. They told her she was welcome to all she wanted. We are told you are more apt to get papers sent in envelopes.

Tomorrow is the day the college students take the oath of service, or whatever it is called. Everything will be closed from 11 until 2. General Wood speaks—it is on the campus east of the Auditorium.

Lots of love from Mother and be a good boy—

France Somewhere
Oct. 6, 1918
My dear Mamma and Nellie,

This is the first chance I have had to write to you for several days, because believe me I have been where it was almost impossible to write. I slept at night or rather tried to, in dugouts that were occupied a few days before by Germans but there is no rest to speak of when you are at the Front. The Bosch were sending over gas shells, just often enough to have to keep awake to put on your mask. High explosive (H.E.) shells and shrapnel shells were breaking just often enough to make it exciting, but at present we are back in rest camps so to speak, but I have seen places that were just a little more restful.

I have slept in my camp bed every night now for over a week and suppose I will continue to use it for some time. The Front is very interesting and believe me you know something is going on there. A good deal of the artillery was farther back than where we were located and noise was unceasing, just a continual roar of cannons and shells going overhead, not only our own shells but Bosch, and believe me the Bosch knows how to handle his artillery.

The villages and towns are all destroyed and just a few crumbling walls are left. Where one of these H.E. shells hits a building there is not much left of it.

Tell Nellie I have seen many Hun helmets and could have gotten any number of them but getting them to you is next to impossible and it is a whole lot of bother to send them, but all that I had to do was to go to where some dead Bosch lay and pick them, as they were quite numerous.

It sure seems good to get with this Division 35 Kansas and Missouri National Guard. There are so many here I know. I have seen a good many of my old friends and it sure seems good to meet them. And the nice thing is that I am assigned and chances are I will remain with this organization during the period of the war. I am now with the Hdqrs. TN. and Mil. Police and I like it very much and so far everything has went just lovely.

But let me tell you it is much harder work and a whole lot less comforts than you get when you are in the S.O.S. I wish that package you sent me would hurry and arrive. I am in need of a watch bad. The one I have won't run, so you see I am out of luck.

How is everything and how is this old world treating you?

I saw Henry J. Allen, of Wichita, our (next governor?) today and had a very pleasant chat with him. He is here doing Y.M.C.A. work but expects to go home soon, providing he is elected and I think he will be.

I did not send a check to you for Aug. and have not drawn my Sept. check yet and don't think I will until the last of this month and will try to send a big check all at once.

As this is all I can think of now will close so write soon.

Lovingly, Harry

OK Lieut. Harry F. Hunt Vet Corps
110 Hdqrs. Tn. and M.P.
Amer. Exp. F.
A.P.O. 743

France Somewhere
Oct . 13, 1918
My dear Mamma and Nellie,

Somewhere in France is right because I don't know how else to put it. We are camped in a forest and I don't know hardly where we are. We were on the march all day yesterday and pulled into these woods after dark last night in a rain and we sure had some job finding a place to stay. Today we are just waiting orders and I think we will be apt to move either this evening or tomorrow, but where we are going I can't say.

This is sure some great life living anywhere and anyplace, but there is one thing we can be thankful for and that is it is not cold, and here is hoping it does not get cold very soon.

This is very pretty country around here. It is hilly or rather mountainous as they call it here and the timber is very pretty. Yesterday when we were on the move we passed through many towns that were all shot to pieces. Take it from me, all that gets in the road of a high explosive shell doesn't last very long. They just simply tear everything to pieces.

We are sure getting good news these days, what little we do get, and I think it will soon be all over because we have the "Hun on the run" and we will keep him moving until he begs for peace. I imagine the U.S. papers are full of this peace dope etc. but the sooner I can come back to the U.S.A. the better satisfied I will be. I have seen all of France I care to see. From now on until next June we are going to have plenty of wet weather.

I thought I saw Lester Stryker yesterday but we were both on the move in opposite directions and I did not get a chance to find out. He is in this division somewhere.

How is college this year? I imagine the old hill is just about deserted, is it not? Will close for this time as I must write to Gussie, so write soon.

Lovingly, Harry

OK Lieut. Harry F. Hunt Vet. Corp.

110 Hdqrs TN. & M.P.

Amer. E.F.

A.P.O. 743

Annie and Nellie received this letter on November 4, 1918.

France Somewhere
Oct. 19, 1918
Dear Mamma and Nellie,

How are you this evening and how is everything treating you? It is cloudy and foggy here tonight. It is trying to rain, but that is nothing uncommon at all for this country this time of year, although yesterday was real nice, and the sun shone part of the day.

We received orders to move just about thirty minutes after I finished writing my last letter to you, and moved that night to this town. Taking all things into consideration we have very good quarters here. We are quartered in an old French town or rather what is left of it, about six kilometers from the Front line (quiet sector) and things are pretty quiet here to what they were at the Front, although the Bosch keep throwing a few shells over here now and then just to let us know they still have a little ammunition left. So far they have done no material damage that I have heard of.

Day before yesterday when I was riding down the road he (the Bosch) started to throw over a few H.E. and let me tell you they sure have some whine to them as they go sailing over. Several of them exploded about 200 yards from where I was and they sure plow the dirt when they go off. However, at that they are not near as close as they were at _____ . We just moved from that place in time. I have been told that the day we left, the Bosch just rained shells into it, but you know you hear so much you never know what to believe.

But thank goodness he has sent no gas shells this way lately and here is hoping he doesn't. I don't like the idea of wearing a gas mask. However, we carry our masks with us all the time, and believe me I can get into mine in nothing flat.

This is very pretty country here in the mountains. The trees are just commencing to take their autumn colors and their colors blending with the dark green of the pine trees make very pretty scenery.

I saw Lester Stryker the other night and had a little chat with him. I say saw him but it was too dark to see anything. We were on the march and I heard someone call his name and I at once got busy and located him and had a little chat with him, but we were on the move and I could not stop long. However, I hope to see him again soon.

We received a card the other day that we could send home for a Christmas box 9x4x3 inches and not weighing more than three pounds, but I gave mine away. I did not think it was worthwhile as I have never received the last package you sent me. I imagine a good many of these will be lost. Wish I would hurry and get some mail. It has been about 45 days now since I have received any mail at all and I need the watch bad, as my other one has gone dead on me. However, I still have my Ingersol and it is keeping very good time.

I took a good bath today and I think I have got rid of all my friends the cooties. Here is hoping so anyhow as they are not the most desirable company there is. From the looks of things I believe the Bosch is getting just about all the war he wants, but let me tell you, the sooner I get back to America the better satisfied I will be and this old war can't end too soon to please me..

Lovingly, Harry

This address:
OK
Lt. Harry F. Hunt, Vet. Corp.
110 Hdqrs. Tn. & M.P.
Amer. E.F.
A.P.O. 743

Annie and Nellie received this letter November 29, 1918.

France Somewhere
Oct. 27, 1918
My dear Mamma & Nellie,

This is Sunday evening and it is a very nice evening and today has been great. The sun has shone most of the time and it has been real nice and warm, just hope it continues that way. How is it where you are and how are you today, wish I would hurry and hear from you again as it has been almost two months since I have received any mail, and you know that is a long time. But such is one's lot when you are moving around so much, but I believe as soon as my mail gets to coming to me here, I will get it more regular. Here is hoping so anyhow.

We are still at the same place where I wrote to you last and everything is going just fine. Now and then Jerry (as we call the Hun) sends over a few shells and about every clear night he comes over in his planes and now and then drops a few eggs so to speak but so far he has done but little damage, and another thing, we have so few nice nights, so he doesn't have much of a chance.

This has been the first clear day that we have seen no air battles but perhaps Jerry is too busy other places to bother us any here. From all reports we get I guess he is being kept pretty busy all along the line. The sooner we can get him whipped so he begs good and proper the sooner the war will end. I think that this winter will just about see the ending of things as the German Empire knows, or soon will know, that their game is up and the quicker they can end things the better off they will be.

I imagine Pres. Wilson's last note to the Bosch told him so he could understand it just what we thought of him and what he will have to do, and what is more he is going to have to do that very thing. Mr. Kaiser must step down from his high roost.

This has been quite a busy day for me, I can tell you. This morning I did my washing and that was some job. There was no other way to get it done so I got myself an old can and boils up so to speak. Also think I am rid of all my friends now (the cooties) cause I took a good bath yesterday and changed clothes, and washed everything today.

How is college this winter? I imagine the old hill is just a little bit deserted, because from what we hear I guess the young men are leaving the U.S. pretty fast. How is Nellie's friend and the Army, or is he over here someplace?

They are certainly throwing over some barrage tonight and we can hear the cannons roar very plainly. We are not far from one of the Fronts where they are doing some pretty hard fighting and we can hear the guns roar very plain. Was out riding awhile this p.m. and visited an old French fort, made modern, and it was very interesting. Some of the rooms were about sixty feet under the ground. Will tell you more about it when I return.

I sent Gussie a clipping the other day about a celebration in Paris and asked her to send it to you so you can learn how the Parisian feels about our recent victories. Wonder how Berlin feels over them?

As this is all I think of right now will close so good night and write soon.
Lovingly, Harry

Annie received this letter on November 30, 1918.

France Somewhere
Nov. 3, 1918
Dear Mamma and Nellie,
...Well I have again been transferred but this time at my own request and I am now with the 130 field artillery, same division and while there is more work I believe I will like it better. One company of this regiment is from Wichita and I have met several former acquaintances although I don't believe the N.G. divisions are as good as the N.A. etc. However maybe it is because I am not used to them and well enough acquainted with them as yet. There are a good many in this division I know.

Received a letter from you and three letters from Gussie this week. Your letter was the one written Sept. 15 on the back of Gene's letter...He is just getting a touch of Army life. Wait until he gets good and used to it...

I was sorry to hear about Uncle Ed's death, but you know such things must happen and death is no respecter of persons. We all must take our turn. One man was killed yesterday from this regiment about a mile below here. He just happened to be where one of Jerry's shells lit and it was his time....

Right now we are located in a forest and my billet consists of a room about six by ten feet, in an old barracks built in the side of a hill. Right outside my door is a tunnel or dugout where we can get if Jerry gets to putting too many shells this way. Yesterday evening he dropped a few big ones around here but they all went further back. But for awhile it seemed like he almost had our post office number.

There has been a dozen air battles over us this afternoon and the anti-aircraft guns have sure been busy, but so far on this Front I have seen no planes come down. We brought three planes down on this Front last week that I heard of. We have had several 340 centimeter (14 in.) naval guns back of us the last few days and they have been sending over some packages for Jerry. Let me tell you they sure shook this old building whenever they were fired. They sure have some concussion I am here to tell you, but you know a thousand pound shell starting on a 20-mile voyage must have some force behind it to move it. I think they are using it or them to fire on a Bosch railroad center a long ways back of the Hun line, and here is hoping they raise a lot of h—l wherever they do fall.

It is very cool and damp here now, but I am fortunate enough to have a small stove in my room which makes it very comfortable. We have candles for lighting purposes and taking everything into consideration we are very comfortably situated.

From what we read in the papers, I guess you folks are enjoying (?) a siege of this Spanish influenza, but you must be careful and not catch it. This is no time for people to get sick. Gussie said in her letter that she was about sick with a cold and thought perhaps she was taking the influenza. Received the sweater vest today from Gussie but your package has not as yet arrived...

We heard several days ago that Turkey had blown up and last night we heard that Austria had done likewise so methinks it is only a question of short time until Germany does likewise. But it is a bitter pill for the Kaiser to take. He started out to rule the world and it looked for awhile like he was going to, but now all his ambitions are shattered and K. Bill's days are numbered. They have commenced to fire the big guns over us, and believe me that sure shakes this shack.

I sent you $300.00 the other day by the Y.M.C.A. and you should receive it in about a month. If you don't receive it by Xmas write Y.M.C.A., 124 E. 28th St., New York and the receipt No. I have is 334410. Will send you the receipt later. Three months of this, $90.00, is commutation of quarters and the rest is what I have saved.

One thing about this life at the Front, you can't spend very much money. Our board costs us 57 cents a day, we eat with the men out of mess tins etc. and our grub is very good but it gets tiresome. We get furnished with fresh beef most of the time when we are in camp but on the move we have Bully beef, corned Willie, etc. The fresh beef comes to us frozen. It is frozen in the states, shipped across in cold storage and kept that way until it leaves for the Front, and it doesn't have time to melt very much.

I am using my knee for a pad to write this on so excuse the writing...
Lovingly, Harry
OK Lieut. Harry F. Hunt
130 Field Artillery
Amer. E.F.
A.P.O. 743

France S.W.
Nov . 10, 1918
Dear Mamma & Nellie,

Sunday night and this has been a glorious old day. Nice and clear and warm, but it has been our first nice day we have had for almost a week, and believe me the mud is getting a fright in this valley. Just hope that it stays nice for a week or so until the mud dries up. Believe me it is far from being pleasant to wade mud all the time.

But you know it is a great (war or) life, if you don't weaken.

One day last week I visited quite a famous city or what has been quite a famous city and where one of the largest battles of this war was fought. While the day was quite foggy and rainy I enjoyed the trip very much. Rode horseback.

Before the war, the city was about 60,000 population and there were many three- and four-story buildings, but now I don't believe there is a building standing that has not a shell hole or two in it and most of them are just a pile of rubbish. This town has never been in the hands of the Bosch either. But I guess they did most of the damage by dropping shells into it and they still do it.

But I don't think Jerry will throw many more shells. I think his game is about lost and if he doesn't sign the Armistice by eleven tomorrow, I think the internal trouble of Germany will cause a complete blow-up. If the reports we get are true, the internal conditons of Germany must be pretty serious. But I always have said that internal troubles of the Hun would end the war because the Kaiser cannot fool them always.

From the sound of artillery around here, one would never think that the war was about over. Believe me, they are sure roaring and now and then Jerry sends a few this way, but I don't believe he sends one for our twenty. But you know that helps to take the pep out of him.

I saw a Bosch aeroplane bring down one of our observation balloons today but none of our men were hurt. I was almost under the balloon and it was an interesting and exciting scene. And the worst part was the Hun got away. But you know that is an everyday occurrence, but it is not often that we see it.

Received two letters from Gussie this or last week mailed about Sept. 15. It looks to me like I soon ought to get some mail again. You know, one letter in two months is not very often. But here is wishing they don't hold us over here long after peace is declared. I have seen all of France I care to see...There is just one Front more that I would like to see, and that is waterfront in good old N.Y. because then it would not take long to get from there home...

I just finished reading the book, "The Martial Adventures of Henry and Me" by William Allen White and I like it very much. There is a whole lot of truth in it and his descriptions are very good. I have been in several of the towns he describes, especially in the Eastern part, and he describes the conditions that exist better than I could...

Lovingly, Harry

FINAL REPORT

OF

GEN. JOHN J. PERSHING

COMMANDER-IN-CHIEF
AMERICAN EXPEDITIONARY FORCES

WASHINGTON
GOVERNMENT PRINTING OFFICE
1920

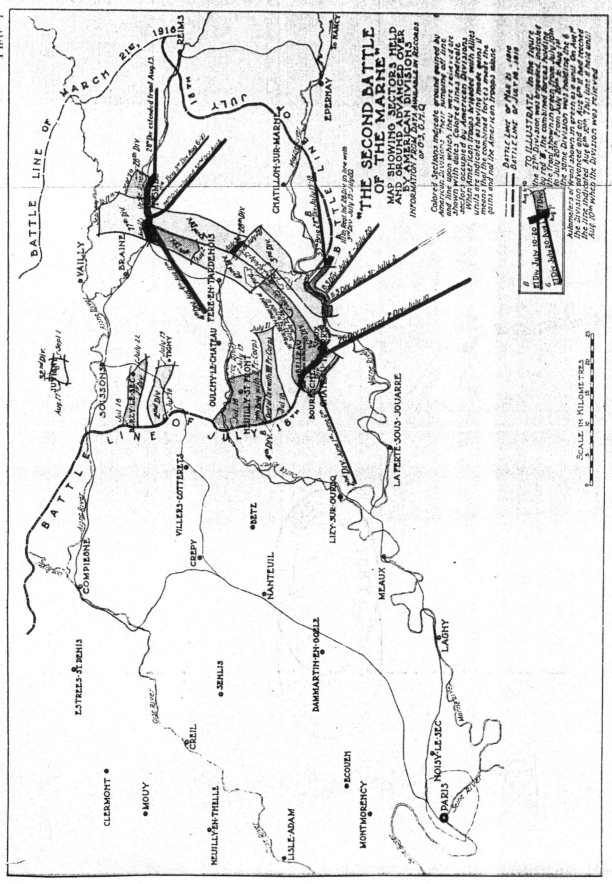

Plate 1

Maps and Flow of Supplies Diagram are from "Final Report of
Gen. John J. Pershing, Commander-In-Chief, American Expeditionary
Forces,"Washington Government Printing Office 1920.

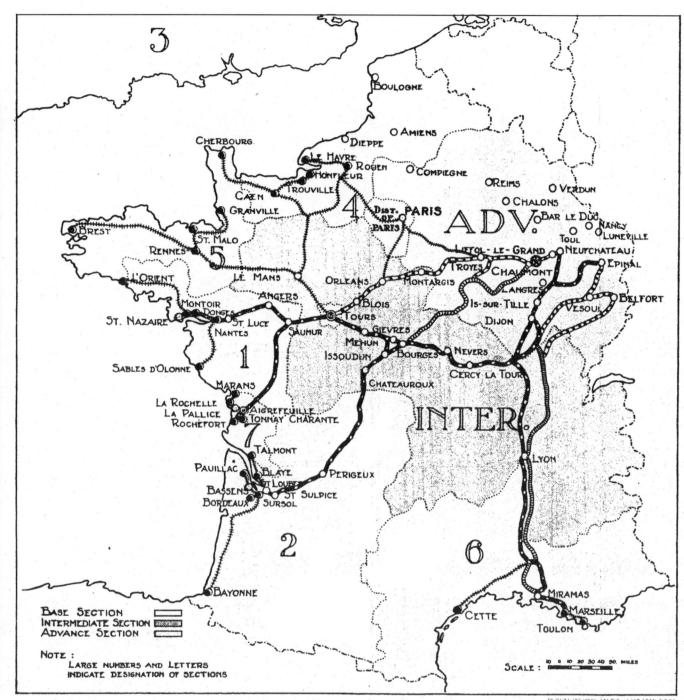

PRINCIPAL FRENCH PORTS AND RAILROADS USED BY AMERICAN EXPEDITIONARY FORCES

GENERAL HEADQUARTERS   HQ SERVICES OF SUPPLY   PRINCIPAL PORTS   SECONDARY PORTS   O IMPORTANT TOWNS

MAIN LINES   SECOND LINES   THIRD LINES   OTHER LINES

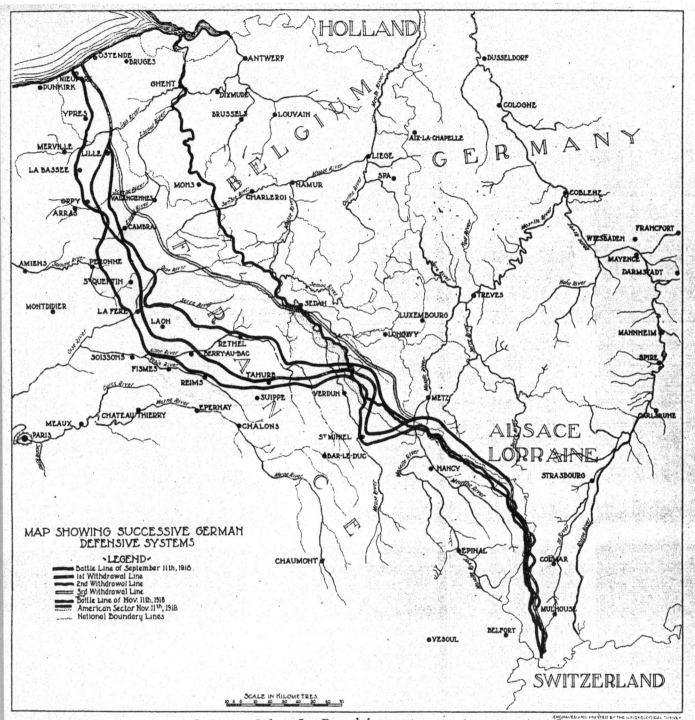

MAP SHOWING SUCCESSIVE GERMAN
DEFENSIVE SYSTEMS

·LEGEND·
— Battle Line of September 11th, 1918.
— 1st Withdrawal Line
— 2nd Withdrawal Line
— 3rd Withdrawal Line
— Battle Line of Nov. 11th, 1918
— American Sector Nov. 11th, 1918
···· National Boundary Lines

SCALE IN KILOMETRES
10 5 0   10   20   30   40   50   60   70

ENGRAVED AND PRINTED BY THE U.S.GEOLOGICAL SURVEY

From "Final Report of Gen. John J. Pershing, Commander-in-Chief,
American Expeditionary Forces."

House Doc. No. 626; 66th Cong., 2d Sess.

DIAGRAM ILLUSTRATING
THE FLOW OF SUPPLIES
IN THE
AMERICAN EXPEDITIONARY FORCES

Requisition on U.S. by C.G. S.O.S.

Purchases in France by G.P.A. for C.G. S.O.S.

45 Day Level

BASE DEPOTS

C.G. S.O.S.

Distributes Supplies into Depots of S.O.S.

30 Day Level

INTERMEDIATE DEPOTS

General Policy

ASS'T C of S G-5 | ASS'T C of S G-1
CHIEF OF STAFF C in C
ASS'T C of S G-4 | ASS'T C of S G-2
ASS'T C of S G-3

15 Day Level

90 Days Supplies in France

ADVANCE DEPOTS

REG. STA. | A | A | REG. STA. | REG. STA. | A | A | REG. STA.

B B B B B B B B B B B B B B

C O N S T A N T   F L O W

1ST ARMY   2ND ARMY   3RD ARMY   DETACHED UNITS

A - Pneumatic Buffer - Storage at Regulating Stations sufficient only to overcome unavoidable irregularity of shipment from Depots and to insure uniform flow at Railheads. Permits no over-accumulation.

B - Railheads. Points at which supplies are delivered to organizations.

From "Final Report of Gen. John J. Pershing..."

House Doc. No. 626, 66th Cong., 2d Sess.

CHAPTER VII

THE 11th HOUR, THE 11th DAY, THE 11th MONTH—THE AFTERMATH

From Veterinary "Military History of the United States," Vol. II, by Louis Merillat, Lt. Col., Vet.-Res., Chief Veterinarian, First Army, American Expeditionary Forces, and Delwin M. Campbell, Lt. Col., Vet.-Res., Editor, Veterinary Medicine, Kansas City Mo., The Haver-Glover Laboratories, 1935.

Page 788:

November Twelfth

"After forty-seven days of unparalleled hell, a million men stood aghast at the terrifying scene. The ground littered with rifles, machine guns, grenades, shells, mess kits, clothing and the miscellaneous belongings of soldiers, told the story of American arms, of the pluck, valor, endurance and sacrifices of the quick-trained American soldier.

"The evidence of a great battle stretched in every direction over the shell-torn ground and shredded forests. What was forbidden ground the day before, was ours now to leisurely explore. The ceaseless flashings and thunder of guns, the chatter, the moans, and the suffering of men, had given way to a pause more impressive than the din of the days now ended. The silence seemed to magnify the ghastly sights reaching to the horizon on every side. The Argonne of that historic day was truly a scene no pen will ever describe nor brush ever paint. Only scenes and action can be written into the pages of history; of sinister Argonne, these arrest the very attempt. On November 12th, the Meuse-Argonne battlefield told more than all historians will ever write to the end of time. One must leave to the imagination what no mind can ever conceive.

"What all of this meant to the United States is as difficult to understand in 1935 as it was on that mournful day of 1918. To the veterinary profession of our country it meant and shall forever mean that on this dark and cruel landscape, the first veterinary corps of our army proved its worthiness in the most difficult military operation of American history..."

ON ACTIVE SERVICE
With The
American Expeditionary Force
Nov. 17, 1918
Dear Mamma and Nellie,

Sunday night and it is a very peaceful, quiet evening and a good deal more quiet than when I last wrote to you, and it has been quiet since last Monday at 11 o'clock. I imagine that the 11th hour of the 11th day of the 11th month 1918 will never be forgotten because at that time the largest war in history ended and it was the first time in over four years that shells ceased being thrown across the battle line.

This old place doesn't hardly seem natural since the roar stopped and we don't hear the mournful whistle of Jerry's shells any more. But I am truthfully glad that it is over and I imagine everyone else is. From all reports, although I have not seen a paper since last Monday, I guess things and conditions in Germany must be pretty bad. I guess starvation and the uprising of the German people had a great deal to do in bringing about the end of the war. But I have always said, as you know, that sooner or later the Hun morale would break, but it must have held together until hunger drove the people desperate.

And now the great question, how soon will we get home, all kinds of rumors are going about. Some think we will be in America by the first of the year 1919 and I only hope they are correct. The sooner I get home the better satisfied I will be.

This old camp is getting mighty lonesome and time is commencing to drag. I think we will leave this camp soon and go someplace where there are better billets. These quarters are far from being pleasant this kind of weather. Every day seems like it is getting just a little bit colder and the last couple of days the mud has not thawed and the ice on the mud holes is pretty thick. But thank goodness we have had no rain since the war ended.

I heard the other day that the Spanish influenza has been causing a good many deaths in America and for some cause or other it has worried me considerable. I trust that everything is allright. Came almost sending you a cablegram but it takes from two to three weeks to get a reply and I hope that by that time I will hear from you. One letter in over two months is not very many you know, and it seems like mail is coming very slow right now, but here is trusting that I soon get some.

Imagine there was great celebrating in America when you received the news of the war ending and there was quite a debate here among we officers just what the people would do. But we are all glad now that it is over and I think that Prussianism is forever erased from the face of the world. The crimes they committed will never be forgotten by civilized nations, nor will they be recognized for years by other nations, for the crimes that they committed are worse than those committed heretofore by any other barbaric nation and they must be made to suffer for their crimes, and suffer in a way that they will remember it...

A few of the French inhabitants of this part of the country are coming back now and I imagine it is a sickening sight to some of them. Some towns where the Bosch artillery was active there is nothing left but ruins. It is hard to tell where buildings once stood. I wonder when they rebuild these towns if they will build modern towns with straight and wide streets or not, but I imagine they will not because you know it is hard to teach an old dog new tricks.

I and everybody else here am having a time with our fires cause we have nothing but green, wet wood to burn and it is a job to get a fire started with it and then to keep it going. It makes one think of the nice warm rooms we have had and hope to have again soon back in dear old America. I usually get run out of my room several times by smoke before I get the fire started.

This is all I think of so will close so write soon.

Lovingly, Harry

130 F.A. (Field Art.)

APO 743

Nov. 23, 1918

Dear Mamma and Nellie,

I did not commence this letter as I usually do, cause we were told we could mention where we were and a few other things. Our present location is Camp Senegalais and I know you can't find that on a map, but it will give you a general location where we are. This camp is about seven or eight miles southeast of Verdun and we have been here now for about a month. Verdun was the town I told you about visiting a week or so ago where the big fight was two years ago.

I was in the first big drive of the Argonne Forest-Meuse River. It was there that I was under shell fire for the first time in my life, but I have told you all about things there in previous letters, even if I did not get to tell you just where I was.

Will give you just a little outline of my journeys in France. I landed at Brest and went from there to Blois via Toursj, then to Bourbonne Les Bains where the L49 came down. It is east and north of Longres, then to Chatillon sur Seine and from there to St. Just Sauvage and Auglure, a couple of little towns north of Rommilly sur Seine. From there I came to the First Army and was assigned to this division. But I cannot tell you the names of towns I have been in and passed through here at the Front because most of them are just ruins and I can't remember the names. But you can get quite a good idea about where I have been, and I will save the rest to tell you, as you know I must have something left to tell you about when I return. From present dope it looks like we are going to be in America in January or February. Believe me, I just hope this dope is true as I have seen all of France I care to. The sooner I can get back the better I will like it, and about everyone else is in the same notion, I believe.

We are sure having nice clear days now. Do you know it has not rained a day since the war ended, although it did try to snow one evening but that was all, just try. Although the days are getting pretty cool, freezes hard every night and does not get warm enough during the day to thaw out, but it seems like every day gets just a little bit cooler.

I am sure glad LaGuerre Finis. I sure would dislike living out this winter. I read the first American newspaper today that I have seen in almost two weeks. From reports in it, Germany is complying with the Armistice regulation pretty good but it was up to her to do so as she was whipped and whipped bad.

Received one letter from you this week, No. 23 written Oct. 6, and its contents were sure read with pleasure. That is only the second letter I have received from you in over two months, and you know that is not very many. Also received one from Gussie written Sept. 30, 1918.

And so Gene did not know where he was going, but I can guess, and if he did sail he won't get to see much of France, I am thinking. I imagine he arrived here just about the time to learn that everything was over and we hear that they are sending them back pretty fast.

Sunday evening, and I will finish this now. A friend came in last night and we talked until bedtime. It is raining tonight and has been at it now for three hours. I had the pleasure of absorbing part of it when a friend and I took a long ride up to Verdun and around some of the hills there where the big battle took place. The destruction is something terrible there, everything being shot to pieces, large hills or young mountains are dug up so it looks like very inch of it has been hit by shells. You can look across the hills and see French graves everywhere. Just looks like they buried them where they fell and that is the way they do. You know almost a half a million men lost their lives in the French army during this battle and the Bosch lost a good many more and from the looks of things you would believe it. But one never seeing the country and the destruction that went on can never realize how bad it really is.

We rode so we could see several square miles of these hills and everywhere we looked it was the same. We did not see all of it by far so you can get some idea just how bad the destruction is.

And so Nellie wants permission to send one copy of the "Stars and Stripes" to her friend, well, as far as I am concerned she may go right ahead, but if he got over here I imagine he will be home before you receive this...Well, this is all for tonight as

I must write to Gussie so good night and write soon.
    Lovingly, Harry
    A.P.O. 743
    130 Field Artillery
    Amer. E.F

Camp Senegalais, France
Dec. 2, 1918
Dear Mamma and Nellie,

    Well, how are you tonight and how is everything treating you? This has been another foggy, cool day but it was too cool or cold for rain and it has been that way now for several days. We are still in the same camp enjoying the mud, to the best of our powers.

    Thanksgiving Day has come and past, and I wonder how you spent the day. We spent it here just the same as we spend any other day and it was a very disagreeable day. I suppose you are wondering what we had to eat that day. We had beef, spuds, gravy, jam, coffee, bread and butter. A very good meal for where we are now, and I suppose everyone is thankful that the Laguerre Finis that the war is over. I know I am and the day that we come back to dear old America will be one of the happiest in my life. I have been in France just a little over eight months and that is entirely too long.

    You know years heretofore I have always eaten dinner that day with you but I am afraid no such luck this year, but from present reports or dope we may be home in January. That won't be half bad will it.

    The day before Thanksgiving I received seven letters so I had something else to be thankful for. One from you, Uncle Billy and Mr. Cory and four from Gussie and believe me every one of them was read with pleasure and every one of them has been answered or will be tonight...

    Yesterday a bunch of the officers from here went up to Fort Duoumont in a truck and looked over the scenery there. This fort was one of the principal defenses of Verdun and was captured by the Bosch and held by them for six months before the French could retake it. Some of the Hun signs and notices are still there. I guess the French are keeping these as a souvenir. Anyhow some of the fiercest fighting of this battle took place right around this fort and the surrounding country sure shows the effect of it. Everywhere you look just shell holes and ruins and it is plain now to see the kind of a struggle that took place there.

    You can see Bosch boots lying around and what is left of the leg still in the boot, also you can see where a good many Bosch fell and what is left of them is still there.

I have a Hun helmet that I picked up after knocking what was left of his skull out of it and will send it to Nellie providing I can get any stamps, but stamps are very hard to find around here.

Tell Mary and Jack hello for me, but say I have played no tennis over here with the French girls, but dodging Bosch shells is just a little more exciting. And you might also add that I still am of the opinion that a (12) judgment is not very good especially when it comes to picking girls for me.

I am glad you enjoy the "Stars and Stripes" and trust that you get them regular. Gussie said that they enjoyed it very much too, especially her mother...

I see by your letter that sis is on the faculty now. How does it seem to be on the inside looking out? Just a little bit different than it was last year I guess.

I am glad to hear you are having things to eat out of your garden and here is trusting that you can make pies before I come back, as you know I have not had any good pies since leaving the U.S. How do they taste...

This is all for tonight so good night and write soon.

Lovingly, Harry

France
Dec. 8, 1918
Dear Mamma and Nellie,

Sunday night and in the same old camp and it is getting lonesomer every day we stay here, but such is life. This week has been fairly nice and we have had very little rain, but the days are damp and foggy and we have very little sunshiny weather.

Was out in the truck today on another sightseeing trip but what we saw is very similar to what I told you about in my last letter. After you see one battlefield they all look alike, but I have seen none yet that could compare with the Verdun battlefield.

Yes, Bourbonne Les Bains is the name of the town where I was but I told you that in one of my letters of a few days or weeks ago. Just as soon as they would allow us to tell the names of towns etc. I received five letters from you this week, No. 25-26-28-29-30 and several from Gussie and one from Frank Petroja and every one of them was welcomed I can tell you. I hope from now on your mail and others that write to me will come through better.

I have not received your package as yet but there is no use to worry about such things. Everyone has the same tale and especially anyone who was a casual. Gussie has been sending newspapers and magazines but they never arrive and I told her to quit sending them. You might just as well do the same, as second-class mail is very slow. You might send the funny papers in letters if you wish as I have better luck in getting letters than anything else, but they are the most important you know. I don't receive as many of Gussie's in proportion as I do yours.

Yes, I imagine you were just a little peeved when you heard that the war had ended and then learned it was not true. I imagine they did celebrate when it really did end. We have heard so many wild rumors that we did not believe that it was over until we heard the guns quit firing and then I think some of the men doubted it for a few days.

Yes, the big question is now when will they send us home, and the sooner the quicker is all I can hope...I mailed a Bosch helmet to Nellie the other day, she can have it until I return. Then I may want it. It came from Dead Man's Hill at Verdun and the Hun that wore it got the full effect of the piece of shrapnel that caved in the helmet and I could have sent part of his skull if it was allowed.

S.O.S means Service of Supply in A.E.F. talk, that is, it is the area from the seaport towns to the advance section, or in other words where the supplies for the army are supplied from.

That was a good letter from the Crown Prince to his dad but I read it a month ago.

Give my best regards to Jack and Isla and the rest of the people there who ask about me, and tell them that I hope to see them soon. Wish I could spend Xmas with you this year, but here is wishing you a Merry Christmas and a Happy New Year. So will close. Write soon.

Lovingly, Harry

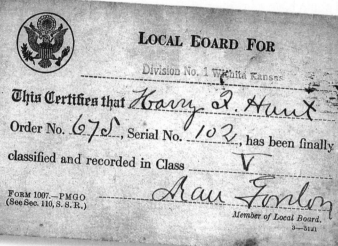

LOCAL BOARD FOR

Division No. 1 Wichita Kansas

This Certifies that *Harry I. Hunt*

Order No. *675*, Serial No. *102*, has been finally

classified and recorded in Class _____ *V* _____

FORM 1007.—PMGO
(See Sec. 110, S.S.R.)

Alan Gordon

Member of Local Board.

3—5141

CHAPTER VIII

THE HOLIDAYS IN CAMP SENEGALAIS

Camp Senegalais
Dec. 16, 1918
My dear Mamma and Nellie,

We are still in the same old place and it is the same old thing every day. With nothing to break the excitement (?) and take it from me, it is one lonesome old place. On an average we get about one newspaper a week so we don't know very much about what is going on in the outside world. There were 18 sacks of mail for this regiment today but only one letter for me from you, and that was written Aug. 25. As you know there was not much news in it.

Sis asked me to send her some copies of the "Stars and Stripes" but I had already done that. But I am living in hopes that I will soon get a bunch of mail as I should now commence to get mail sent to me to this regiment. Some here have received mail sent as late as Nov. 26 from Kansas.

The package has never arrived and I have given up all hopes of ever getting it. We heard today that the Armistice had been extended one month and from all appearances now I don't hardly think we will get home as soon as I thought some time ago. But believe me I sure would like to leave this country and especially this mudhole. It has rained almost every day since I last wrote, and we seldom ever see the sun. Don't think I am a chronic grouch, but I am just a little bit out of sorts today.

I am glad Nellie enjoyed her visit with her friend. He does not know what he missed by not getting to come over across the pond. As one hears a good many say, I would not take a thousand dollars for my experience but would not give a dime to go through it again. But such is life, you know.

President Wilson is over here someplace we hear but that is about all we know. I am in hopes that in their conference they will send part of us home soon and that I will be in that part. I have a couple of souvenir vases, the kind made out of cannon shells with the fancy engraving and want to get a couple more. Did think I would try to send them but guess I will wait and bring them. I am glad you received the checks and you should have that I sent by the Y.M.C.A. now.

Wonder what you are planning on doing Christmas. Only wish I could come and spend it with you but just as soon as I can, Gussie and I will be up to see you, and you don't know how much I wish it was this year. Anyhow I will think of you and am sending my best wishes for a Merry Christmas and a Happy New Year.

I want you folks to excuse this letter, but it is the best I can do under the circumstances as this monotony is sure getting tiresome...

Lovingly, Harry

Camp Senegalais France
Dec. 21, 1918
Dear Mamma and Nellie,

Well, this is the end of another long old week, with but very little excitement to break the monotony and plenty of rain and snow to make it very disagreeable. It has rained every day since I last wrote to you and has snowed a couple of times, but not very much and the snow has just about all melted. It is getting a good deal cooler.

I suppose you have all your plans made for Christmas and I have too, but I wish I could come and be with you. But here is hoping I soon will be, but I don't know a thing about how soon we will leave for home.

We have been sending around to some of the big towns trying to get a few extras for our mess and the men's mess and the one truck went to Car lu Duc but I don't think they got very much. The men are working on an entertainment and that will be about the end of our Christmas festivals. We are trying to get a Y.M.C.A. entertaining company here for next week and here is hoping we succeed because this is certainly one lonesome place.

From all appearances now I will not be with this regiment much longer as this regiment is being motorized. Just hope they make a casual out of me and send me home, but all of the horse-drawn organizations are getting more horses and they are good American horses they are getting. You see this regiment is 155 C.M. (6 in.) cannons and is supposed to be motor-drawn. They have been using horses and will now change and from appearances they will go to Germany...

I may take a seven-day leave some of these days, but have not made up my mind where I want to go. I am thinking some of going to Lyon or Nice. Would like to spend

86

the whole time in Paris but we can't go there on leave. A good many are getting their Xmas boxes and a good many are not, and some just get the label without any package. This is all I think of tonight so will close so write soon.

Lovingly, Harry

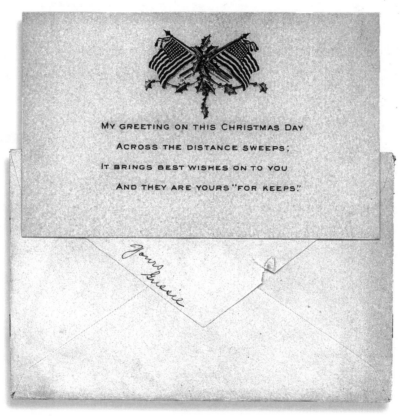

MY GREETING ON THIS CHRISTMAS DAY

ACROSS THE DISTANCE SWEEPS;

IT BRINGS BEST WISHES ON TO YOU

AND THEY ARE YOURS "FOR KEEPS."

Yours Gussie

Among Us Are

Col. Hugh S. Brown
Lt. Col. W. W. Thurston
Maj. Thomas H. Jennings
Capt. James C. Hughes
Capt. Rollin Ritter
Capt. Victor J. Wagoner
Capt. Fredric H. Olander
Chaplain Earl A. Blackman
Lieut. Dana T. Jennings
Lieut. Frank H. McFarland
Lieut. Clay McClellan
Lieut. Harry H. Vaughan
Lieut. Roberts J. Schroeder
Lieut. Joe F. Major
Lieut. Harold G. Newton
Lieut. ~~Harold~~ Davis Mike j
Lieut. Hugh M. Davison
Lieut. Joseph S. Kemper
Lieut. ~~Arthur~~ F. Hunt. Harry
Miss. Elizabeth Marshal
Miss. Irene Dayton

Christmas at Sénéglais

December 25th 1918.

Day M. Phelan
Rollin Ritter
W.M. Thurston
T.J. Jennings
W.J. Rassell
Jno. F. Jennings
James C. Hughes
Jos. S. Kimper
Hugh McDavisson
Robert J. Schroeder
Frank Stanley
Michael J. Davis
Harold H. Newton
Aug. H. Brown

PROGRAMME de EATS

Olives   Cornichons

Soupe Creme de Tomates

Dinde Rotie Vermont

Coupe de Noix

Pommes Puree

Petit Pois Juin a la Creme

Mais au Beurre

Gateau de Chocolat

Amandes   Bonbons

Chocolat

Cigares   Champagne

Camp Senegalais, France
Dec . 29, 1918
My dear Mamma & Nellie,

'Tis Sunday night and I will answer your two good letters that have come to hand this week. One was dated Nov. 23 and one was Nov. 30. I also received the views of Camp Funston dated Dec. 4...

Well, Christmas has come and gone and I wonder what kind of a time you had. We had a very good time and a very good dinner. We now have an officers' mess and we were fortunate enough to get a couple of turkeys (French) and they sure tasted good, I am here to tell you.

We also had the pleasure of having a couple of Y.M.C.A. ladies (girls) here with us that day. They are serving chocolate here in the regiment and that day we had them to mess with us and we also had something for dessert that I know you folks did not have.

We almost had a white Christmas. It snowed about two inches the night before but most of the snow melted before the next day. Then we had rain and it has been raining all week and most of the time pretty steady. Believe me, it is sure tiresome this wading mud. But we have hopes of leaving here soon and the present dope has it that we are going to LeMans (S.W. of Paris) and from there to America! I just hope that it is true.

I now have my trunks with me and I am certainly glad of it as I was needing some of the things in them. One of the officers here went to Gievres after them and brought them as far as Lerouville. I went down there in a car and got them, also went down to Commercy the same day. We followed right along the Meuse River and went through St. Mihiel and several other towns that were once held by the Bosch. Part of the towns are all shot to pieces and others are not so bad off. St. Mihiel is not shot up near as bad as Verdun. You can no doubt see these two towns on the map and I have been pretty well over the ground in between the two towns.

We have had a couple of Y.M.C.A. companies here since Xmas entertaining us, one this p.m. and one Friday. Believe me, they were sure good and we certainly enjoyed them. The first time I had seen a show since in September and this week you might say is the first time I have heard an American woman talk since in September.

You folks can imagine how a fellow gets over here in these out of the way camps especially here at what was the Front 11-11-11. I never in all my life saw such a lonesome place and I sure hope we are getting out of here soon. I still have hopes of leaving this country for the good old U.S.A. in the next two or three months.

From all reports we hear I guess President Wilson is sure having some time over here. Glad someone is. I guess Gene and Nellie's man are glad to get home, but I imagine Nellie's friend would have enjoyed coming across. If I get to come home soon

I won't have anything to complain of outside of a few hardships. The experiences I would not take a whole lot for, but would not give anything to go through it again.

Not long until 1919 and here is wishing you a happy and prosperous New Year and ere long I hope to see you. Well, must close and write to Gussie so will bid you a fond good night and sweet dreams. Write soon.

Lovingly, Harry

130 F.A. A.P.O. 743.

From Veterinary Military History of the United States, Volume I, published in Chicago, U.S.A., Veterinary Magazine Corp., 1935, pages 559-560:

"December, 1918.—Of course, following the Armistice there was widespread demand for demobilization in all branches of the army, and veterinary officers were no exception to the general rule in besieging the War Department for discharge and petitioning Senators and Representatives from their home districts to bring this about. Demobilization, a stupendous task, began at once. By the end of the year, about 400 veterinary officers, who had urgent reasons for returning to civilian life, were discharged, but the large number of animals the army possessed and the inevitable delay in disposing of them prevented any general discharge of the veterinary personnel."

Annie didn't receive this letter, written January 5, 1918, until February 10.

Camp Senegalais
France
Jan. 5, 1919
My dear Mamma and Nellie,

'Tis Sunday afternoon once more and I will try to write you a few lines in answer to your letter of Nov. 12, which I received day before yesterday. That is all the mail I have received this week or since last writing to you. I can't understand why I don't get more mail. Others here get mail sent as late as Dec. 20 and your letters should come to me here to this regiment now, and never a one comes. I don't hear from Gussie either, but then I guess I am one of the unfortunate ones over here, when it comes to getting mail. But then I keep living in hopes that I will soon hear from you again and that my luck will change soon. Here is hoping that it will change to the good, 'cause it could not get much worse.

Must say that was sure some celebration the people of Manhattan had when "La Guerre finis" or rather when the Armistice was signed. For me here at the Front, that 11-11-11 will never be forgotten as long as I live. The deathly quiet that existed when we had been hearing the continual roar of the guns, especially that morning when it seemed that everything was a roar. But I will tell you more when I return, but when that will be I cannot say.

I don't think I will be with this regiment much longer as it is to be motorized, and some of the motors are here now. Wish they would make me a casual and send me home, but I am afraid that won't happen as we are getting too many horses over here. But I should worry, guess they will send me home sometime.

It is still raining - yet - that is, by spells, and the wet or rainy spells are way ahead in the percentage column, although the sun has shone a little this past week.

New Year's Eve Mrs. Booth and a couple of men gave us a little show under the auspices of the Y.M.C.A. Mrs. Booth is of Salvation Army fame and sometimes called "the little mother" in the U.S. but I have seen shows I enjoyed just a little more. We like the shows that have plenty of pep best, you know. Then after the show we put on a little watch party, but Mrs. Booth and company were too tired to stay long. We welcomed the New Year in with a hearty respond, that is, the best we could do under the circumstances.

Sure wish I could have had the pleasure of eating that meal with Jack and Isifa. Tell them I said hello and that I will be ready for a good square meal when I do return to the good old U.S.A.—God's country, as we call it over here.

And so, Mamma, you think this will be the last war, well, you know the old saying that great minds don't always run in the same channel. I think there will be wars just as long as this old world is run or tried to be run by human beings, because there is too much animal nature in the people of the world not to fight, and every war will get worse in proportion to the education and knowledge of the people, as modern means of slaughter will always lead.

As this is all I think of will close, O yes, do you ever hear from Gussie. So keep on writing and maybe I will get one of your letters now and then.

Lovingly, Harry

Hdqs. 130th Field Artillery,
American Expeditionary Forces,
31 December 1918
A.P.O. 743

From: Harry F. Hunt, 2nd. Lieut. V.C. U.S.A.

To   :   Chief Veterinarian, (Thru Channels)

Subject: Personal Report

       Report myself on duty with the 130th Field Artillery, 60th Brigade the
entire month of December.

                                    2nd. Lieut. V.C. U.S.A.

                                        Headquarters 35th Division
                                        American Expeditionary Forces
                                        6th January 1919.

Special Orders)
   No. 6   )
                              Extract.

*   *   *   *

     2.   Second Lieutenant Harry F. Hunt, V.C., Unit No. 8, 35th Division, attached to 130th Field Artillery, is transferred to Unit No. 10, Veterinary Corps, assigned to 69th Infantry Brigade.

     3.   Farrier Budd W. Skaggs, Veterinary Corps, having reported to this Division for duty is assigned to Unit No. 4, Veterinary Corps, 35th Division, attached to 110th Engineer Train.

     4.   Private Roy Wimmer, Veterinary Corps, Unit No. 8, 35th Division, attached to 130th Field Artillery, is transferred to Unit No. 4, Veterinary Corps, 35th Division, attached to 110th Engineer Train.

     5.   Private Troy I. Warren, Veterinary Corps, Unit No. 8, 35th Division, attached to 130th Field Artillery, is transferred to Unit No. 3, Veterinary Corps, 35th Division, attached to 110th Ammunition Train.

*   *   *   *

                         By Command of Brigadier General Dugan:

                                   H. S. HAWKINS
                                Colonel, General Staff,
                                    Chief of Staff.

OFFICIAL:

      WM. ELLIS
      Lt. Col., Inf., U.S. Army
        Division Adjutant

Copy to -
            Lt Hunt
            C O, Vet Unit #8
            C O, 130th F A
            C G, 69th Inf Brig
            C O, Vet Unit #4
            C O, 110th Engr Tn
            C O, Vet Unit #3
            C O, 110th Amm Tn
          Div Vet
          Personnel

Lt. Hunt

Headquarters 137th Infantry
January 12,1919

From; 2nd Lt. Harry F. Hunt V.C.

To;   The Commanding Officer 69th Brigade.

Subject; Condition of Animals in 137th Infantry Regiment.

    1. The general condition of animals in this Regiment
is very good. Grooming is being done very well, but there is
some dust in the animals coats. The stables are being kept
in very good condition, such as they are, but many of the
stables are very poor, being damp, dark, and poorly ventilated,
and very unsanitary.

    2. Some of the animals show that the fetlocks have been
clipped recently, but this has been discontinued, and under
no condition, unless permission is given, will the fetlocks be
clipped.

    3. The shoeing of many of the animals is very poor, owing
principally to the lack of proper sized shoes. Many of the mules
are shod with large French pattern horseshoes, as there are no
Mule shoes available. Would recommend that a supply of horse
and mule shoes be procured at once.

                                    Harry F. Hunt

CHAPTER IX

WITH THE 69th INFANTRY BRIGADE

Sampigny, France
Jan. 11, 1919
Dear Mamma and Nellie,

Just a few lines tonight as I am not feeling any too good principally because one of my wisdom teeth is hurting, but think it will be allright in a few days.

I am now with the 69th Infantry Brigade and we are located now about twelve kilo. north of Commercy and about the same distance south of St. Mihiel. This brigade is made up of the 137 and 138 Infantry Regiments and there are a good many here I know but have not been around enough to see many of them...

The 130 F.A. is being equipped with motors but I was glad to get away from the mudhole although I have much more to look after here, as both supply companies are horse- and mule-drawn.

We are quartered here in French houses or parts of houses and have very good quarters but it is hard to get enough wood to keep warm by. Don't know whether we are coming home soon or not, some days we hear we are and then we hear we are not. But I still have hopes of being with you in the spring. Will close for tonight so good night and write soon.

Harry
69 Infantry Brigade
A.P.O. 743 A.E.F.

Annie received this letter on February 10, 1919. It was written on Knights of Columbus Overseas Service stationery with the K of C emblem.

A.P.O 743
Jan. 19, 1919
Dear Mamma and Nellie,

Sunday night again and for a wonder today it has hardly rained, for which we are very thankful. Believe me, we enjoy these few days now and then when we don't get any moisture to speak of.

Well, how goes everything with you tonight and how is this old world treating you? For a change I am feeling fine considering everything, but just a few of the things are pretty hard to take into consideration. Received three letters from you this week and the same from Gussie. Two of yours were mailed in Sept. and one Oct. 1, 1918, and Gussie's were from Sept. 20 to Sept. 30 but they were all welcomed even if they were just a few days behind the times. Others here have been getting mail dated Dec. 30 but such is my luck.

One of these letters from you was written principally by my little sis and I think it must of been a short time after he left as she was certainly cranky and gave me a good lecture about a few things I had done, but principally about things I had not done, and about a few words being misspelled.

I am going to take this opportunity to inform the dear lady that some of her dope really amused me and that I kinda enjoyed reading it.

Just keep the good work up, because her long, scratched-up letters keep me busy for some time deciphering them and help make or start fires very well. I might further add that it is a good thing that none of her letters are opened by the censor. He would sure think he had a code letter or one written in a language unbeknown to the civilized world. You have no doubt heard the song, "O Brian Trying to Speak Hawaiian" and I have heard several American soldiers trying to parle vous Francais but I have yet to meet someone who can butcher any language as my college professor sister can the American lingo. I also might add that if she does not like the way I write and tell things and a few things I don't tell, why just try coming over here herself and eat corn, Willy and Bully Beef, hardtack and a few other favorite dishes we have, and see if it is not good for her chronic stomach trouble due to not getting enough exercise since her strolling partner is away.

I sure feel sorry for some poor man and I feel it my just and rightful duty as one man to another to write and inform him of his condition before it is too late. If I am not too tired when I get through I will.

Yes, I have heard of the town of St. Just Sauvage but don't hardly understand how you thought of it. I spent about two months there. Yes, Paris is a very beautiful place and I enjoyed my visit while there but take my advice and don't come there on your honeymoon, as Paris is chuck full of pretty French girls and someone might forget all about you—believe me these French girls are crazy after Americans.

I am also very much pleased to learn that you think the apron is cute and cunning. I suppose that ere this time your favorite Maltese kitten has almost wore himself and the apron out trying to tear it away from around his dear little neck. In closing I wish to say that if by chance I have forgotten to mention anything, why just don't worry and fret cause I will try not to.

I intended to ride over to some of the old Bosch trenches back of St. Mihiel today but was too busy otherwise, but want to go over there some of these days. I have been kept pretty busy ever since coming to this brigade testing the animals for glanders and have about one more week's work ahead of me before I am through. Then I will try to take a few trips around close.

I was down to Commercy this morning and tried to buy a watch but they wanted too much money for them. So I am still without a watch, but hope to go to Nancy or Toul soon and think I will have better success there.

Have not heard a thing yet about coming home but still have hopes of being there this spring sometime. The sooner the better is all I can say. I am tired of living like we do here, although I guess we should not complain. I imagine there are a few places that are just a little bit worse. Say, maybe you think I would not enjoy being in a good warm room once more with someone there to cheer me up.

You asked a good many questions in your letters but I think I have answered them all in previous letters so will bring this to a close. So good night and write soon.

Lovingly, Harry

Annie and Nellie received this letter on March 3, 1919.

Sampigny, France
A.P.O. 743
Jan. 26, 1919
Dear Mamma & Sister

Sunday evening and I wonder what you are doing to pass the time away. This is sure some night over here, I am here to tell you, and it is not getting any better fast. This week has been very cold and but little rain has fallen. Tonight it is trying to snow and acts very much like it would succeed and if it does snow now, it will stay on the ground because everything is frozen.

This has been a very busy week for me. I have the entire brigade to look after and they are scattered out a good deal. I have the 137th and 138th Infantry Regiments, the machine gun companies and the 129th machine gun battalion and each one is about twelve kilo apart so you can see I am kept pretty busy. I ride horseback all the time, and while I enjoy the riding it is not so fast as a car.

Just finished mallium testing the entire brigade this week and got one reactor and that means that I must test this regiment every seven days for the next month so I guess I will be kept pretty busy.

I forgot to tell you in my last letter about seeing Mr. Felphs (how do you spell his name) here the other day. He is a sergeant in some engineering company and they are now located near Commercy. You know his father is the butcher at Schaffer's and he was captain of the 1913 football team, or I guess the 1912 team. It sure seemed good to see him and we had quite a nice chat.

I received a letter from you today, No. 20 written Sept. 18. We hear by all kinds of dope that we are soon to leave this area and go to LeMans and there wait our turn to go home. Just hope it is true. I would certainly enjoy being in good old America and to be free to do as I pleased once more. I still have hopes of being with you sometime this spring.

I have about three months pay now, and if we don't get orders to leave soon, think I will send it to you. I have been holding off as there are some things I want to buy before leaving this country. I have also been thinking quite seriously of taking a leave since I have never taken a leave since being over here and we are entitled to seven days every four months, but it is not accumulative.

However, the time I spent in Paris was just like a leave. I would like to go there again but it is out of the leave area due principally to the lack of food there. Of course, every one would go there if they got the chance...

I have never received any of the magazines you have sent to me or the box and no late letters but such is my lot...

Lovingly, Harry

Feb. 1, 1919
Sampigny, France
Dear Mamma & Nellie,

Saturday night and 'tis a very cold night and this week has been very cold with a little snow mixed in. Just about two inches of snow is all that has fallen so you can see we are not suffering on account of snow. However, the cold is very disagreeable here because we have no warm place to go or to stay. The rooms are very airy due to so many shell holes in the house and everything being so well ventilated but I am sure glad it is not as cold here as we hear it is in the U.S.A., and especially Kansas. From all reports I guess you are having one of the coldest winters in history. I am hoping your coal is holding out and that you are keeping warm. Take it from me I am not very warm.

Received three letters today, one from Nellie, Jan. 3, one from Billy Jan. 7 and an advertisement. First mail I have had for a long time but it is about time. Wish I would hurry and hear from Gussie, sometimes I think maybe flu is the trouble. But then the mail service is punk. Your last letter I received was Dec. 4 and where are all the ones in between, but such is life.

I am glad you received the helmet. It is from "Dead Man's Hill" near Verdun and I could have sent part of the Bosch's skull if I thought you wanted it, but I think I described that hill and conditions there to you in a former letter, did I not.

And so Nellie kinda thinks something is going to happen about the middle of Feb. Well, I can't imagine what she means unless she is going to be married and I kinda expected that. All I can say is that I am sending my best wishes etc. but not to wait for me to be there. Also not to forget our little wager we made several years ago. I think it was ten boxes of something, but then I always knew I would win, but I am not saying what may happen toute de suite after I return to the U.S. and get my discharge. From present dope I think we will soon be in the U.S. because we (this Div.) has orders to leave here or be ready to leave by Feb. 7 for LeMans and if those orders are not changed, or me not transferred, it means we are homeward bound and I will certainly be glad to be back in the good old U. S. A. again. So let us hope that the orders are not changed.

As it is very cold here and news very scarce I will close, so write soon. Excuse my mistakes because I have to stop every few minutes and warm my hands. So you can readily see I am writing under difficulties.

Lovingly, Harry
69 Infantry Brigade
A.P.O. 743

With the war over at last, Harry was anxious to return to his work with the Southwestern Serum Company in Wichita. On February 5 he wrote a memo to request to be transferred to the U.S. and honorably discharged.

American Expeditionary Forces,
5th February 1919.

From: 2nd Lt. Harry F. Hunt, Vet.Corps (attached 69th Inf. Brigade)

To: Commander-in-Chief, American E. F. (thru military channels)

Subject: Resignation.

    1.   I hereby request that I be immediately transferred to the
United States and honorably discharged upon arrival.

    2.   Before entering the United States Army, I was engaged in the
manufacture of Anti hog cholera serum, a serum for the prevention of hog
cholera, and was financially interested in the Southwestern Serum Company,
Wichita, Kansas.   I intend to resume my duties with this Company as
soon as discharged from the Service. It is necessary to commence
preparations in the Spring in order to insure a successful business year
in this business.   In recent statistics given by the Bureau of Animal
Industry, the annual loss in Hogs dur tothis disease was fifty million
dollars, and for this reason believe that my services are of more value
for the conservation of meat in the United States than they would be in
this country.

    3.   Took examination June 30, 1917 for commission in Veterinary
Corps at Manhattan, Kansas. Commissioned 2nd Lt. V.C. July 20, 1917.
Ordered active duty September 18, 1917.   Arrived in France March 26, 1918.

                                        HARRY F. HUNT

Manhattan Kansas Feb. 7-1919.

My dear Harry-

This is such a cold
stormy evening, compared with the
weather we had last month. it snowed
some last night, and froze hard,
several nights in January, it did not
freeze at all, these sudden changes
are what make us feel the cold so.
I've been cold all day, the wind is
from the east, and the kitchen and
dining-room are so hard to heat, but
the bed-room is nice and warm. I
wonder if you have plenty of fuel
and are warm. I imagine you have
plenty of covers at night, those
blankets are so warm. This is Farm
and home week at the college, there
are a good many strangers in town,
I have been attending some of the lectures

and demonstrations, yesterday, and last evening a woman from England lectured, and it was most wonderful and dreadful, the things she told us. Mrs and Mr Jim Clark and Mrs Polson of Fredonia were here Sunday, they drove up to see Izil and Roxie Clark, they were two days coming up, but hoped to make better time going home. Everything about as usual in Fredonia. Mary Polson is some-where in the east, taking some kind of school training, they asked about you. Nellie saw Mrs. Schubert today, asked if Harry was home. Jesse Corsaut was here last evening, he was discharged a few days ago, and was here visiting, looked fine in his uniform, we talked about all the boys and wondered where they were, and what they were doing. Merle is here about every evening, so you see we have plenty of company. Sunday Feb. 2nd was ground hog day, you know they say if he comes out and sees his shadow, he goes back and stays six weeks, as there will be six more weeks of winter but if it is cloudy, he will stay out, and winter is over, well, he saw his shadow, so we can expect more winter, we are getting more eggs since the snow has gone, we got five one day, they are forty two cents now, so I imagine everyone is getting more. We went down town today, and had nellies invitations, will keep yours, for you will send yesina one, no one here but relatives, haven't

heard if Uncle Billy is coming, nellie and Merle have gone to the Basket Ball game. K.S.A.C. plays K.U. again tonight, we beat K.U. last night, also there is a ball tonight, after the game, and they are going, plenty to go to, but I do not enjoy it so much, nellie is going home with Merle tomorrow and come back Sunday night. We are wondering where you are, if you are on your way home, etc, etc, The flu, is about gone here, some pneumonia, Flora wrote Mgr. Liggett had committed suicide — shot himself with a shot gun, he had raised nothing, and was so worried, he told the neighbor, he had nothing to feed his cattle, guessed he would shoot himself, but they did not think he meant it. This is all now hope you are well, and on your way to, M.S.A.
Lots of love
mother,

(Author's Note: The score of the basketball game on February 6, 1919, was Kansas State Agricultural College 33, Kansas University 30. The following night the score was KSAC 41, KU 27.)

From Mrs. A. Hunt
1010 Bluemont Ave
Manhattan Kansas.
U.S. Agrattors.

Deceased Eff grattors
Capt Inf. N 50

Lieut, Harry _____ Hunt. Vet. Corps
69 Infantry Brigade
American Ex. Forces
France.

A. O. 749

MANHATTAN
FEB 8
7-30P
19   19
KANS.

UNITED STATES POSTAGE
3 CENTS

DECEASED
STATISTICAL DIVISION A.E.F.

erican Expeditionary Forces

Officers Mail
O.A.S.

Knights of Columbus
OVERSEAS SERVICE

FROM *A. S. Hunt N.C.*
69 Inf. Reg. APO 743
A.E.F.

PASSED AS CENSORED ✶ 2081

POSTAL EXPRESS SERVICE N°743 27 JAN 1919 MILITARY

OK
A. S. Hunt
A. C.

Mrs. Annie A. Hunt
1010 Plemmon Ave
Manhattan
Kansas
U.S.A.

CHAPTER X

"I'VE BEEN COLD ALL DAY"

Manhattan, Kansas, Feb. 7, 1919
My dear Harry-

This is such a cold stormy evening compared with the weather we had last month. It snowed some last night, and froze hard. Several nights in January it did not freeze at all. These sudden changes are what make us feel the cold so. I've been cold all day. The wind is from the east, and the kitchen and dining room are so hard to heat, but the bedroom is nice and warm.

I wonder if you have plenty of fuel and are warm. I imagine you have plenty of covers at night. Those blankets are so warm.

This is Farm and Home Week at the college. There are a good many strangers in town. I have been attending some of the lectures and demonstrations. Yesterday and last evening a woman from England lectured and it was most wonderful and dreadful the things she told us...

Nellie saw Mrs. Schubert today, she asked if Harry was home. Jesse Corsart was here last evening, he was discharged a few days ago, and was here visiting. Looked fine in his uniform. We talked about all the boys and wondered where they were, and what they were doing.

Merle is here about every evening, so you see we have plenty of company. Sunday Feb. 2nd was Ground Hog Day, you know they say if he comes out and sees his shadow, he goes back and stays six weeks, as there will be six more weeks of winter. But if it is cloudy, he will stay out, and winter is over. Well, he saw his shadow, so we can expect more winter.

We are getting more eggs since the snow has gone. We got five one day. They are 42 cents now, so I imagine everyone is getting more. We went down town today and got Nellie's invitations. Will keep yours for you. Will send Gesina one. No one here but relatives. Haven't heard if Uncle Billy is coming. Nellie and Merle have gone to the basketball game. K.S.A.C. plays K.U. again tonight. We beat K.U. last night (author's note: the score was 33 to 30), also there is a ball tonight after the game, and they are going. Plenty to go to, but I do not enjoy it so much. Nellie is going home with Merle tomorrow and come back Sunday night.

We are wondering where you are, if you are on your way home, etc. etc. The flu is about gone here, some pneumonia. Flora wrote Myrt Liggett had committed suicide—shot himself with a shotgun. He had raised nothing, and was so worried he told the neighbor he had nothing to feed his cattle, guessed he would shoot himself, but they did not think he meant it.

This is all now. Hope you are well, and on your way to U.S.A.

Lots of love,

Mother

Was it the bitter wintry wind, penetrating the very pores of her frame home, that chilled her to the bone that day, or was it a foreboding of the tragic news to come?

N. 48
Manhattan, Kansas
March 3, 1919
My dear boy—

Your very welcome letter of Feb. 1st came today and we were mighty glad for it, I can tell you. Am glad too that you have one letter, if not the others, so maybe they will come to you by and by. One of our letters to you, dated Nov. 2nd, came back Thursday. It had a blue pencil marked base hospital No. 8, so there must be other Harry Hunts over there, and I imagine there is where your box with the ring, watch and sweater is. I would like to tell the other fellow what I think of him. He surely knows what mail belongs to him and what does not. There was a Capt. Hicky in France from Manhattan and not one bit of mail did he get, or none from his wife, while he was in France. He is home now. So many are coming home, and we hope to see you soon.

Had a good long letter from Gussie. She is well, said she wrote you every other day, and sometimes every day, and I am like you, I cannot understand why you do not get at least a few. She sent several pictures of Neva Marie, her mother and sister. Said she was fleshier than when I saw her. I answered *it and asked why she could not send one of her pictures so I could see how she looked. Neva Marie is a little dear, and I can almost hear her calling that Negro "chocolate drop."*

Mr. and Mrs. Austin have gone to Hot Springs, Ark. Mrs. has not been very well lately. Nellie and Merle are on the farm and are getting along fine. I wrote you about them before.

Nell is here. Wm. went to Fredonia, has his old job back at the brick plant at $150 per month. I do hope he likes it and stays. He will be glad to know you have his letter. He asked a couple times if you ever said anything about getting his letter.

We had a blizzard last Thursday night. The wind blew a gale, and it snowed, got dreadful cold, but it is pretty warm now, and the snow about all gone. We had very cold weather the last of Dec. and the first weeks of Jan. but with the exception of a couple cold spells it has not been so bad. Am sorry you are so poorly housed, and hope you will be more comfortable when this reaches you.

We received the money you sent Nov. 1st and wrote you about it, also the helmet. Are getting enough eggs to use these days.

We have a message from Washington saying Harry F. Hunt had died Feb. 6th from gas. We doubted it, because we wondered what you would be doing with gas now. We wrote to Washington, and sent a cable to France to the Major of your company, and as yet have had no reply, but we are very hopeful.

Aunt Flora has not been very well, but is better. We are well and hope you are.

The letter was not signed.

This was the 48th letter Annie wrote to her son, but he died before it reached him. It was returned marked "Deceased."

Even before Annie wrote to her son on March 3, she had sent a cable to the major at the 69th Infantry Brigade Headquarters in France, asking for verification of his death, and received a personal reply from Major C. B. Robbins in March, 1919.

In April she received a letter of condolence from J. M. Cory, an official of Harry's former employer, The Southwestern Serum Company.

Annie was a subscriber to "Woman's Home Companion" magazine. In her desperate attempts to obtain information about her son's reported death, she wrote to the editor of the magazine and received a reply written June 29, 1919.

After the magazine's editor contacted The American Red Cross officials in an effort to assist Annie in locating and communicating with the chaplain who officiated his burial service in France, she received a letter from the Red Cross National Headquarters. It gave the names of the chaplains who had served the 69th Infantry Brigade, but the Red Cross made no attempt to locate them, as they had returned to the United States.

Here is Harry's obituary as hand-written by Annie:

"Harry Frank Hunt, son of Frank M. and Annie S. Hunt, was born at Fredonia, Kansas, Nov. 9, 1890. Harry finished the 8th grade at a country school in Wilson Co. then his mother and sister with him moved to Manhattan where Harry graduated in the Veterinary course in 1913. He was employed at Wichita, Kansas by the Southwestern Serum Company. Upon the declaration of war he volunteered, and was sent to Camp Pike Arkansas, and the following March was sent to France.

"Lieut. Hunt was connected with the 69th Brigade headquarters, of the 35th Division. He was a skilled veterinarian and had charge of the livestock of this regiment. His death occurred at Sampigny France Feb. 6, 1919. He had been asphyxiated by fumes from a charcoal fire, the post mortem examination showed. The funeral occurred at Commercy, France and the body laid at rest in a little cemetery near the field hospital at Commercy. The body was brought to the U.S. July 3rd 1921 and buried at Fredonia, Kansas by the side of his father who had died in 1901."

Lt. Hunt was 28 years old.

HEADQUARTERS
SIXTY-NINTH INFANTRY BRIGADE
A.E.F. France, 3rd March, 1919

Mrs. Annie S. Hunt,

        Manhattan, Kansas.

Dear Madam:

        Your cablegram asking for verification of the
death of Lieut. Harry F. Hunt was received this morning
at these headquarters and I want to send a cablegram to
the Red Cross to be sent to you, as follows:

        "Lieutenant Harry F. Hunt died February 5th,
        1919, accidental charcoal gas poisoning."

I knew Lieut. Hunt quite well during the short time that
he was with these headquarters as Brigade Veterinarian and
was unexpressably shocked to hear of his sudden death.
Charcoal has been used as fuel, to a limited extent, in
the stoves in the officers' billets. Lieut. Hunt had been
having a touch of Influenza or a bad cold and was staying
in his quarters. The stove had been filled up with charcoal and Lieut. Hunt apparently laid down upon his bunk
and gone to sleep. The pipe was partly choked and the gas
given out by the charcoal was sufficient to cause his death
while asleep. His body was found only a few hours after
death occured and there were no signs of a struggle and
apparently his death had been very peaceful.

        I assure you that I feel a personal loss at the
death of Lieut. Hunt, as he was not only a competent and
efficient officer, but a manly and agreeable friend as well.

        I saw him only the day before his death occured.
He had been assigned to the 137th Infantry, which is one of
the regiments of this brigade, stationed in the town of
SAMPIGNY and he done splendid work in caring for the animal
transportation of that regiment. We all felt a sense of
personal loss at his death.

        I am glad to be able to write you these few lines
concerning the cause of his death, which was determined by a
medical post-mortem autopsy. It is apparent that the death
was accidental.

                        Sincerely yours,

                        C.B.Robbins

wlk   Major, Adjutant, 69th Inf. Brigade

WILL E. McCLURE, D. V. S.
CHIEF VETERINARIAN

J. M. CORY, PRESIDENT

F. J. RATHMAN, SEC'Y & TREAS.

The Southwestern Serum Co.

U. S. VETERINARY LICENSE NO. 56

MANUFACTURERS OF

**HIGHLY POTENT
ANTI-HOG CHOLERA
SERUM AND
VIRULENT VIRUS**

OFFICE PHONE: MARKET 1012
NIGHT PHONES
F. J. RATHMAN, MARKET 1320
J. M. CORY, MARKET 6266

SOUTHWESTERN
SERUM
SAVES
SWINE

IOWA STATE PERMIT NO. 21
OKLA. STATE PERMIT NO. 8

WICHITA, KANSAS   April 12, 1919.

Mrs. Anna F. Hunt,

Manhattan, Kansas.

Dear Mrs. Hunt:

Under separate cover we sending you this morning's Eagle
which contains an article in regard to Harry's death.

I wish to say that his acquaintance here was quite large
and his many friends regret very much that he has passed away.
This company and its officers ask you to kindly accept our
condolences.

Harry has some stock here in safe in the Wichita Zinck
Mining Co., however, ⊥ regret very much that at present time
it doesn't look very valuable. But I assure you that anything
that is done with the company in regard to selling its assets
or stock that Mr. Fred Rathman and myself will see that Harry's
share goes to you. If you desire we will mail the stock to you.

Yours very truly,

J. M. Cory

JMC:B

WOMAN'S HOME COMPANION

THE CROWELL PUBLISHING COMPANY

OFFICE OF THE EDITOR   381 FOURTH AVENUE, NEW YORK

June 29th, 1919.

Dear Companion Reader:

Your letter was received at this office after Mr. Phillips had left France for this country, having completed his work for the Red Cross.

Mr. Phillips was fortunate enough to put through a plan of cooperation between the Army and the Red Cross that has resulted in a very large percentage of definite reports. Practically all of the investigation has either been completed or is under way, and the records are being sent back to this country as rapidly as possible under the direction of the Army.

Your letter has been forwarded to Washington, where Mr. Phillips assures us it will have the most careful attention.

Sincerely yours,

THE EDITORS.

THE AMERICAN RED CROSS

NATIONAL HEADQUARTERS

WASHINGTON, D.C.

BUREAU OF COMMUNICATION

W. R. CASTLE, JR. DIRECTOR

Mrs. Annie S. Hunt
1010 Bluemont Ave.
Manhattan, Kans.

Lt. Harry G. Hunt
Vet. 69th Inf.

July 7, 1919

My dear Mrs. Hunt:

        The following report comes to us from E. Ronan, GHQ Chaplain,
with the request that we advise you of its contents:

        "Relative to the chaplain who had charge of the 69th
Infantry Brigade last February I submit the following information:
In the 69th Brigade there were two regiments, the 137th and 138th, in
each of which were three chaplains. The following are the chaplains on
duty with this Brigade Feb. 6th:

Chaplain H.V Fox,	)	
" A.J. Sawkins	)	137th Infantry
" W.E. Sullens	)	
Chaplain E. A. Shearer	)	
" C. R. Terry	)	138th Infantry
" Thos. F. Ripple	)	

        This Brigade has returned to the States so I am
afraid it would be rather difficult to locate the chaplains.

                Signed: E. Ronan
                        QHG Chaplain   "

        We are indeed sorry that at this time it seems impossible for
them to locate the chaplain for whom you made inquiry.

                Yours sincerely,

CLW/FB

                W R Castle Jr
                W.

Harry's death, even more shocking because it came after hostilities had ceased, was a devastating blow, not only to Annie and Nellie, but to Annie's other relatives. Her nephew, Ralph Brindle, who was six years old, made the trip from Fredonia to Manhattan with Annie's sister, Flora Brindle.

"I never knew your Uncle Harry," Ralph, then in his 80s, said in a telephone conversation in 1996. "My earliest recollection of Nellie was my family went to Manhattan and visited with them and your parents announced their engagement.

"I remember being at your grandmother's house when she had the plaque with a blue star on it that indicated she had a son in the service. Later the blue star was replaced with a gold one."

He recalled that Annie had received a letter from Harry saying he was going to LeMans to wait for a boat to come home. About two days later she received the telegram from the War Department that he had died. Aunt Flora and Ralph went to Annie's to console her.

"Here she was—the war was over. Her son had come through it. He was safe. Then the telegram came. It was the worst possible situation you could think of as far as a mother. I can remember her being grief-stricken and Aunt Flora and I trying to help her," Ralph said. "Both Annie and Flora were devastated with grief."

In spite of her broken heart, Annie could not ignore her compassion for other families who had lost loved ones in "the war to end all wars." She would not ask for the special favor of having her son's body returned unless the same could be done for others.

Nearly two years passed. Then one day Annie saw in the newspaper that the bodies of American deceased would be returned home. On January 5, 1921, she wrote to the War Department in Washington, D.C., and asked that Lieut. Harry F. Hunt's body be sent to Fredonia, Wilson County, Kansas, in care of her brother, George S. Brindle, so he could be buried in his hometown cemetery.

Months of official paperwork, telegrams, and letters later, the necessary arrangements had been made and Lt. Hunt was returned to "God's country". Along with some of his countrymen from midwestern states, Lt. Hunt was returned to Hoboken, New Jersey, the port from which he had embarked, on the S.S. Cambrai, and from New York City to Omaha, Nebraska, on the Chicago, Rock Island & Pacific Railroad. He was taken from there to Fredonia, Kansas, on the Missouri Pacific Railroad.

Tech. Sergeant James J. German, Quartermaster Corps, and Private First Class Matthew Greaney, 18th Infantry, were the escorts for the deceased to Omaha.

Some of the documents from The National Archives tracing that procedure are reproduced here, along with a list of other men who were returned at that time.

Lt. Hunt's final funeral service was held on the Court House lawn in Fredonia on Sunday, July 3, 1921. The Rev. J. Ashton Davies officiated the ceremony. Interment was in the Fredonia City Cemetery with the Charles Walter Post, American Legion, in charge.

RG 92, Records of the Office
of the Quartermaster General

I do not want my sons remains brought to the U. S. unless in some future time all the bodies are brought and buried in a national cemetery, then I would want his brought with the others, and buried in a national cemetery here.

Very Truly yours,

Mrs. Annie S. Hunt.

4th Ind.

Hq 137 Infantry, American E.F. March, 25th, 1919. - To: Commanding
Officer, Base Hospital, No 91. Commercy.

1. Forwarded. Lt Hunt's body was removed from Sampigny where
he died to your hospital at Commercy where an autopsy was held.

By order of Lt Col. O'Conner.

GUY G. BRATTON.
Capt. 137 Infantry.
Personnel Adjutant.

1-incl.

5th Ind.

O.C.O., Det Patients Base Hospital No.91 Commercy (Meuse) 4 April 1919
To: Headquarters 137 Infantry American E.F.

1. Returned.   On or about 7th February 1919 the body of deceased
Harry F.Hunt 2nd Lieut., Vet. Unit 130 Field Artillery was brought to
this Hospital for autopsy only.

2. The autopsy   was performed and findings were reported to you under date
8th Feb.1919 (Carbon   monoxide poisoning as cause of death)

3. Regimental Chaplain receipted for the body and held funeral services.

4. We have no records of this Officer except findings of autopsy
and the location of the grave which has been inserted on the blank attached
hereto.

David F.Caddell,
2nd Lieut., S.C.
Registrar.

DFC/jab

Co

253

Manhattan Kansas
Jan. 5th 1921.

To The War Department,
Washington D.C.

I see by the papers the
bodies of our boys are being sent home
from France. When the body of my son
Lieut. Harry F. Hunt Vet. Corps is sent
please have it sent to Fredonia, Wilson
County, Kansas, care of G. S. Brindle,
as that is our old home and his
father is buried there.

Very Truly Yours
Mrs. Annie S. Hunt,
1010 Bluemont,
Manhattan
Kansas.

Hunt, Harry F.

2⁵³

Jan. 14, 1921.

FILE

293.8-Cem. File #95060 (Hunt, Harry F., 2nd Lieut.)

From: The Quartermaster General, U. S. Army, (Cemeterial Division)

To: Mrs. Annie S. Hunt, 1010 Bluemont, Manhattan, Kansas.

Subject: Return of Body.

1.   In reply to your letter of January 5, 1921, requesting that
the remains of your son, the late 2nd Lieut. Harry F. Hunt,
Veterinary Unit, 130th Field Artillery, be returned to Mr. G. S.
Brindle, Fredonia, Wilson County, Kansas, for private interment,
you are advised that instructions will be issued that your wishes
be complied with provided there is no relative whose legal right
to direct disposition has priority over yours.

2.   This office regrets that it is unable to state at this time
when this particular case will be reached. However, in order
that sufficient time may be had in which to make the desired
arrangements in connection with the final burial, the legal next
of kin will be notified by telegram from Hoboken office upon
receipt of information from Europe that the remains have been
shipped, and again upon shipment of the body from Hoboken, New
Jersey.

3.   Your attention is invited to the enclosed Cemeterial Division
Bulletin, No. 10-F-W, which gives in detail information concerning
the work of returning the remains of our soldier dead.

        By authority of the Quartermaster General:

                                      CHARLES J. WYNNE,
                              JF   2nd Lieut., Q. M. C.   HW

MAILED

JAN 1 5 1921

G.R.S.

G.R.S. Form No. 120
Shipping Inquiry
(Ed. of Jan. 1, 1921)

61⬡6   ho

WAR DEPARTMENT
OFFICE OF THE QUARTERMASTER GENERAL OF THE ARMY
CEMETERIAL DIVISION
WASHINGTON,
Hoboken, N.J.

MAR 23 1921

R

FROM: Chief, Cemeterial Division, O.Q.M.G.

TO: Mrs. Annie S. Hunt, 1010 Bluemont Ave., Manhattan, Kansas.

SUBJECT: Remains of 2nd Lt. Harry F. Hunt. Vet.Unit 130th F.A.

The records of this office show that you have requested that the body of the above named _____

soldier be returned to the United States and shipped to Fredonia, Wilson Co.,

Kans. c/o G.S.Brindle. _____ *no change cms*

If these are not the correct instructions, please correct them. Make corrections on reverse side of this sheet.

The nearest next of kin may choose between (1) return of body to any address in the United States; (2) interment in the National Cemetery, Arlington, Va., or any other National Cemetery; or (3) body to remain in Europe.

By authority of the Quartermaster General.

CEMETERIAL DIVISION

GEO. H. PENROSE
Colonel, Q.M.C.

If all blank spaces below are not filled out, it will necessitate a return of this paper and a SERIOUS DELAY in the shipment of this body. State in each case WHETHER or not these relatives are STILL LIVING.

MAR 31

Was soldier married? *He was not*

NAME OF	NO. AND STREET	TOWN	STATE
Soldier's widow *none*			
Soldier's children. (Name oldest first) 1. *none*			
2.			
3.			
Father *died 1901*			
Mother *Annie S. Hunt*	*1010 Bluemont*	*Manhattan*	*Kans.*
Brothers, (Name oldest first) 1. *none*			
2.			
3.			
Sisters. (Name oldest first) 1. *Nellie E. Converse*	*Route 4*	*Eskridge*	*Kans.*
2.			
3.			

Date *March 29-1921*   Signature *Mrs. Annie S. Hunt*

Address *1010 Bluemont, Manhattan, Kans.* Relationship *Mother*

Important - CAREFULLY read instructions before filling out this paper

S-1947/MB   (over)

Manhattan Kans, May 29 1921

I, the undersigned, am the <u>Mother</u> and nearest living next of kin of
(Relationship)
the within-named soldier, and desire the following disposition of his remains, viz:
(Strike out all except the one showing the disposition desired.)

1. As stated on first page of this sheet.

2. To be returned to the U.S. and shipped to <u>*G. S. Brindle*</u>
(Name)

   (R.R.station) <u>*Fredonia,*</u>   <u>*Kansas,*</u>
(State)

3. ~~To be returned to the U.S. and buried in~~ _____ ~~National Cemetery.~~

4. ~~To remain in Europe, for burial in a permanent American Cemetery.~~

   Signature *Mrs. Annie S. Hunt.*

INSTRUCTIONS FOR FILLING OUT.

1. If definite instructions for the disposition of a body are not received from the next of kin within two weeks of its arrival at New York, burial will be made without further notice in the World War Section of Arlington National Cemetery.

2. The transfer of bodies will be made ENTIRELY at Government expense.

3. This paper MUST BE SIGNED BY THE PERSON WHO IS THE NEXT of kin IN THE ORDER shown in the square on the other side of this sheet.

4. This paper must be returned showing the name and address of each of the nearest next of kin in the spaces provided therefor on the other side of this sheet.

5. If there are minor children of the deceased soldier and no widow, the LEGALLY APPOINTED GUARDIAN of the children should ascertain their wishes and act for them in this matter.

6. If YOU are not the nearest next of kin, please ask the nearest next of kin, if living near you, to fill out this paper.

7. If YOU are not the nearest living next of kin and do not know who or where the nearest relatives are, please fill out this paper AT ONCE and mail to this office

8. You are requested to return this paper AT ONCE in order to avoid delay in the case of this body.

9. Use the inclosed envelope-pay no postage.

Note:-INSTRUCTIONS FOR THE DISPOSITION OF REMAINS will be issued by this office upon the properly executed authority of the legal next of kin in each case. The widow is the first person having disposition of the remains of her husband. Should there be no widow or children, the father and, in turn (upon his decease), the mother, is the proper authority. The brothers, in order of seniority, and then the sisters in order of seniority, if there are no brothers, rank next in authority to decide. Under an opinion rendered by the Judge Advocate General of the Army, if a widow has remarried she forfeits her right, and the next of kin as given above will make decision.

S-1947/MB *The reason I am asking the body shipped to Fredonia is, Fredonia is our old home, and my husband is buried there. G. S. Brindle is my brother, and an uncle of Harry F. Hunt.*

Very Truly Yours
Annie S. Hunt

April 26, 1921

File No. 293.8 Cem.Div.Cor.Br.
(HUNT, Harry F.)

Mrs. Annie S. Hunt,
1010 Bluemont Ave.,
Manhattan, Kansas.

Dear Madam:-

This is to advise you that your wishes will be complied with and the body of your son, the late Second Lieutenant Harry F. Hunt, Vet. Unit 130th. Field Artillery will be returned to the United States and shipped to you in care of G.S.Brindle, Fredonia, Kansas.

About ten days before the arrival of the body in the United States you will be notified by telegram and requested to confirm the above shipping instructions. You should immediately reply to such telegram, to avoid delay in the shipment of the body.

The Department desires to convey to you assurance of sympathy in your bereavement.

By authority of the Quartermaster General:

R.E.SHANNON,
Captain Quartermaster Corps,
Officer in Charge.

By-

J.F.BUTLER,
Captain, Infantry

SR.TMW

SPECIAL ORDERS   June 27, 1921.   se
NO.   152.   - E X T R A C T -

x   x   x   x

3.   Under the provisions of paragraph 87, Army Regulations, Tech.
Sergeant James J. Gorman, Quartermaster Corps, and Private First Class Matthew
Greaney, 18th Infantry, as escorts will proceed from Hoboken, N.J., to Omaha,
Nebraska, accompanying the remains of the following deceased soldiers onroute t
destinations set after their respective names:

Pfc. Arthur E. Stuckey, 2395407, Co. A, 7th Inf.   Ansley, Nebr.
Wag. Cloll Hiser, 2222961, Sup. Co., 358th Inf.   Arkansas City, Kans.
1st Lt. Lester S. Hart, 11th Aero Sqdn.   Aurora, Nebr.
Pfc. Herman L. Bond, 2905779, Co. G, 355th Inf.   Benkelman, Nebr.
Pfc. Gerald A. Bowen, 84315, Co. A, 168th Inf.   Chariton, Iowa.
Pvt. Clyde Edward Philpott, 2830014, Co. F, 359th Inf.   Creston, Iowa.
Pvt. Frank E. Carlson, 100473, Co. C, 163th Inf.   Fontanelle, Iowa.
Pvt. James A. Holden, 164940, Co. E, 14th Engrs.   Kansas City, Mo.
Pvt. Ben Johnson, 86345, Co. D, Sig. Corps, 3 Bal.Sq.   Kansas City, Mo.
Pvt. Joseph Liebman, 2200587, Co. G, 354th Inf.   Kansas City, Mo.
Pvt. Jasper Turman, 488915, Co. E, 64th Inf.   Kansas City, Mo.
Pfc. Jesse Surrena, 84443, Co. Mil.Spec.Co.1st Depot.Div   Sheridan, Wyo.
Pvt. Paul Nagel, 246103, Co. F, 28th Inf.   Staplehurst, Nebr.
Pvt. Albert L. Anderson, 1461833, Co. K, 140th Inf.   Agenda, Kans.
Pvt. John C. Hinrichs, 2104495, Co. D, 23rd Inf.   Atlantic, Ia.
Pvt. Charles G. Fulton, 2190574, Co. B, 353rd Inf.   Cuba, Kans.
Pvt. Henry H. Kasha, 2189966, Co. G, 353rd Inf.   Cuba, Kans.
Sgt. Poo P. McHugh, 101987, Co. K, 168th Inf.   Cumming, Iowa.
Cpl. Lawrence E. Lindblom, 2151142, Co. C, 39th Engrs.   Des Moines, Iowa.
Pfc. Herman L. Funks, 3308939, Co. D, 350th Inf.   Herkimer, Kans.
Sgt. Harold E. Weber, 1472275, Hq. 110th San.Trn.   Lincoln, Nebr,
Pvt. Chas. Ernest Redd, 2202732, Hq. Co., 335th Inf.   Norton, Kans.
Pvt. Lewis W. Jennings, 2113101 Co. C, 353rd Inf.   Smith Center, Kans.
Pvt. Delbert D. Powell, 2853455, Co. G, 358th Inf.   Walnut, Iowa.
Pvt. Paul Paulsen, 2849438, Co. G, 358th Inf.   Council Bluffs, Iowa.
Pfc. William A. Hall, 2192179, Co. A, 353rd Inf.   Winfield, Kans.
Cpl. Clayton C. Miller, 1467038, Hq. Co., 130th.F.A.   Wichita, Kans.
2nd Lt. Harold W. Chance, 2nd Corps School.   Wichita, Kans.
Pvt. Charles L. Hunt, 2197576, Co. H, 353rd Inf.   Bigelow, Kans.
Pvt. John Evans, 490046, Co. D, 34th Inf.   Cedarville, Kans.
Pvt. Arthur J. Stenger, 2197283, Co. C, 356thInf.   Council G. Grove, Kans.
2nd Lt. Harry F. Murk, 7th Unit, 130th F.A.   Fredonia, Kans.
Pfc. William F. Summers, 1033624, Co. G, 64th Inf.   Goffs, Kans.
Pfc. Victor Krebaum, 2213703, Co. L, 355th Inf.   Great Bend, Kans.
Pvt. Alvin E. Randolph 489617, Co. G, 56th Inf.   Creighton, Mo.
Cpl. John R. Westling, 2176901, Co. G, 353rd Inf.   Green, Kans.
Cpl. Clarence C. Hinkley, 2206439, Co. E, 356th Inf.   Kansas City, Kans.
Pvt. Glenn Seaver Livingston, 2206735, Co.C, 356th Inf.   Kanapolis, Kans.
Cpl. Roy R. King, 2239469, Co. C, 315th Wire Co.Sig.Corps. Lamar, Mo.
Pfc. Percy H. Arnold, 1457488, Co. I, 139th Inf.   Latimer, Kans.
Pvt. Emile Sommerla, 74875, Co. C, 3rd Amm. Trn.   Fort Leavenworth, Kans
Cpl. Harry F. Joyce, 2175981, Co. C, 353rd, Inf.   Leavenworth, Kans.
Pfc. Chester McDonald, 2175349, Hq. Co., 353rd Inf.   Longton, Kans.
2nd Lt. Scott L. Lennen, Att. D.Co., 23rd Inf.   Lyons, Kans.
Pvt. Charles C. Jones, 2146772, Co. C, 30th Inf.   Neosha Rapids, Kans.
Pvt. Gomer W. Dempsey 1445486, Co. C, 110th Amm. Trn.   Nevada, Mo.
Mech. Charles H. Hanlin, 2176110, Co. D, 353rd Inf.   Osawatomie, Kans.

Pvt. John M. Graham, 2250013, Co. H, 358th Inf.   Owasso, Okla.
Pvt. Alvin Myron Graham, 73rd Co., 6th Marines (120209)   Oxford, Kans.
Pvt. Norman E. Lovell, 2198563, Co. D, 341st M.G.Bn.   Springfield, Nebr.
Cpl. Turley E. McCloskey, 2175602, Co. A, 353rd Inf.   Beloit, Kans.
Sgt. James H. Teel, 2220449, Co. L, 358th Inf.   Bartlesville, Okla.
Pvt. Elbert F. Mills, 2846556, Co. K, 355th Inf.   Akron, Iowa.
Pvt. Fletcher Lawrence Farley, 51st Co., 5th Marines,   Bancroft, Nebr.
Pvt. Edgar W. Smith, 3071872, 462nd Co., M.T.C.   Beaver, Iowa.
Pvt. Leopold Good Thunder, 3127679, Co.D, 128th Inf.   Belvidere, S.Dak.
Pvt. Ray Henry McVay, 79th Co., 6th Marines, (305741).   Clearwater, Nebr.
Pvt. George Fuerst, 976124, Med. Det., 117th Amm. Trn.   Kaylor, S.Dak.
Pvt. Ivar E. Holsten, 1427459, Bty. F, 19th F.A.   Lyons, Nebr.
Pvt. John J. Halweg, 486908, Co. E, 34th Inf.   Merrill, Iowa.
Pvt. Charles O. Powell, 2846158, Co. I, 355th Inf.   Neligh, Nebr.
Pvt. Silas Kitto, 2847153, Co. G, 354th Inf.   Niobrara, Nebr.
Pvt. Harold M. Oxley, 490315, Co. E, 64th Inf.   Paton, Iowa.
2nd Lt. Will C. Severson, M.G.Co., 356th Inf.   Sioux City, Iowa.
Pvt. Arthur E. Whiting, 3808415, Combat Officers Depot.   Sioux City, Iowa.
Pvt. John S tekelenburg, 119888, Hq. Co., 6th Marines   Sioux City, Iowa.
Cpl. Dan Bryan Racobs, 2182403, Co. M, 355th Inf.   Smithland, Iowa.
Cpl. Julius H. Lafrenz, 2182278, Co. K, 355th Inf.   Tekamah, Nebr.
Pvt. Ralph A. Piper 2847354, Co. B, 355th Inf.   Wood Lake, Nebr.
Sgt. Henry Teigeler, Jr., 2181252, Co. A, 355th Inf.   Fremont, Nebr.
Sgt. Edward H. Larson, 2182034, Co. H, 355th Inf.   Genoa, Nebr.
Pvt. George S. Palmer, 2847944, Co. K, 355th Inf.   Grand Island, Nebr.
Cpl. George S. Rosencrantz, 2182037, Co. H, 355th Inf.   St. Edward, Nebr.
Pfc. John Clyde Lowder, 2197343, Co. E, 354th Inf.   Brunswick, Mo.
Sgt. Glen M.Read, 2181356, Co.B, 355th Inf.   Shenandoah, Iowa.
Cpl. Ira V.Swanger, 215933, Co. F, 130th Inf.   Persia, Iowa.
Pvt. Helmer E. Reyelt, Co. K, 16th Inf.   Harlan, Iowa.

     Upon arrival at Omaha, Nebraska, escort will deliver the aforesaid remains to the Depot Quartermaster, that city, for distribution to their respective homes and upon completion of this duty will return to Hoboken, N.J., and report to the officer in Charge, Rail & Cemeterial Branch.

     The Transportation Service will furnish transportation covering journey of escort from Hoboken, N.J., to Omaha, Nebraska, and return and covering shipment of remains from Hoboken, N.J., to destination set after each name. The Finance Service will pay escort a per diem allowance, in advance, at the authorized rate (4 rations plus $.50), for five (5) days as provided in paragraph 1223-(g) Army Regulations, it being impracticable for the Government to furnish subsistence in kind. The journey is necessary for the public service. (Q.M.C.-Cemeterial)

x   x   x   x

2 AGA
1 CO of Escort
1 Capt. VanVliet
1 Depot Quartermaster, Omaha, Nebr.
89 Capt. Shannon
1 File

By order of Colonel BRADLEY.

JOSEPH A. MARMON,
Lieutenant Colonel, Infantry.
Executive Officer.

LIEUT. HUNT DIES

Lieutenant Harry F. Hunt, formerly with the Southwestern Serum company, 2202 North Lawrence avenue, died in Sampigny, France, February 6, from asphyxiation. He had
repaired to his billet for the night,
leaving a charcoal stove burning, and
it was reported that he was overcome
by gas fumes.

Mr. Hunt removed to Wichita in
1915 from Manhattan after he was
graduated from the Kansas agricultural college to accept a position with
the serum company. He enlisted in
this city in May, 1918, and was later
sent to France. After the cessation
of hostilities, he was transferred to
the 137th infantry of the 35th division as a veterinarian of the officers'
reserve corps.

As an officer and man, Lieutenant
Hunt had commanded the respect of
his men and his ability in discharg-
ing his duties won for him the esteem
of his fellow-officers and those of
higher rank. In Wichita and at college he made numerous friends who
heard the announcement of his death
with regret.

The deceased is survived by his
mother and sister, residing in Manhattan, the late lieutenant's former
home. He has no relatives in Wichita.

* * *

DEATH OF HARRY F. HUNT

Former Aggie Student Was Killed By Monoxide Gas

Confirmation of the reported
death of Lieut. Harry F. Hunt, K.
S. A. C. '13 has been received in
Manhattan through a letter received by Mrs. C. T. Gist, from her
brother, Lieut. H. G. Newton. Lieut.
Hunt's mother, Mrs. Annie Hunt,
who lives at 1010 Bluemont received a telegram a few weeks ago
from Washington saying that her
son had died of monoxide gas, Feb.
6. Mrs. Hunt had heard from her
son under date of Jan 26, and later
received a letter from him dated
Feb. 2 both showing up to be on
duty and well. The letter from
Lieutenant Newton reveals that
Lieutenant Hunt had taken sick
with the influenza on the 6th dying
that night. Post mortem examination revealed the cause of his death
as the gas fumes from the charcoal
that was burned in the fireplace in
his room.

Lt. Harry F. Martin was in the
Vetinary Corp serving first with the
Artillery and at the time of his
death, with the Infantry near Commercy, France, where he was given
burial. He leaves beside his mother, a sister, Mrs. Merle Converse of
Eskridge.

UNTY CITIZEN

DEATH OF FORMER FREDONIAN

Lieut. Harry Hunt Killed by Charcoal Fumes.

Word was received last week by
Fredonia relatives of the death in
France, of Lieut. Harry Hunt, which
occurred February 6th. A letter from
a comrade to Harry's sister, who with
her mother is living at Manhattan,
contains the following information
concerning the tragic occurrence:
Lieut. Hunt took sick the afternoon
of the 6th, and was found dead in his
billet that evening. A post mortem
revealed that he had been suffocated
by fumes from a charcoal fire in the
fireplace. He was buried in the Commercy cemetery.

The deceased was the only son of
Mrs. Frank M. Hunt, of Manhattan—
formerly Miss Anna Brindle, of Fredonia.

He was born in this city November
9, 1892. In 1898 the family moved to
Colorado. In May, 1891, his father
was accidentally killed in a gold mine,
and the mother with her son and
daughter, returned to Fredonia where
they resided for some time. Later
they moved to Manhattan, where
Harry was graduated from the agricultural college in 1913. Since then
he has been connected with the South-
ern Kansas Serum Co., of Wichita,
until he volunteered for service. He
had been in France about a year, and
was with the 69th Brigade Headquarters, 35th division. He was a
graduated veterinarian, and was highly esteemed by all who knew him for
his ability and many sterling traits
of character.

Lieut. Hunt was a nephew of Will
and George Brindle, of Fredonia, and
of John Brindle, who lives northwest
of town.

His mother has the deepest sympathy of many Fredonia and Wilson-
co. friends, in this second tragic bereavement in her life.

ANOTHER BODY FROM OVER-SEAS TO BE BROT TO FREDONIA

The body of Harry Hunt, who was
2d lieutenant in the veterinary corps,
is expected to arrive in New York
from overseas, June 15th, and will be
brot to Fredonia for burial. His mother, Mrs. Hunt, lives in Manhattan,
and he was a nephew of Geo. Brindle,
and Misses Nellie and Flora Brindle,
of Fredonia. Funeral arrangements
will be announced later.

SOLDIER'S BODY HERE SOON.

The body of Lieutenant Harry Hunt,
a former Fredonia boy, will be returned to Fredonia for burial, probably
some time next week, according to
Dr. E. C. Duncan, post commander of
the American Legion here.

Lieutenant Hunt is the son of Mrs.
Anna Hunt, was educated as a veterinarian at the state agricultural college, and became known thruout the
state for his research studies into
problems affecting the live stock of
the state. He was a member of the
veterinarian corps in France when he
was taken ill and died.

The service here will be in charge
of the American Legion.

OBITUARY

Lieut. Harry F. Hunt, of the Veterinary corps, attached to the 137th Infantry, was found dead on his bed in his billet in Sampigny, Thursday evening, shortly after 6 o'clock. He had been asphixiated by fumes from a charcoal fire, the postmortem examination developed.

Lieut. Hunt had not been feeling well, and went to his room after dinner and lay down. He was not discovered until several hours after death. The funeral occurred Sunday at Commercy; an escort of officers of the regiment, and a platoon from the First battalion attending the funeral. His body was laid to rest in the little cemetery near the Field hospital at Commercy.

The Lieutenant was connected with the 69th Brigade headquarters. He was a skilled veterinarian, and had charge of the live stock of this regiment. He was popular among all who knew him, and his death is sincerely mourned. His home was at Wichita, Kans., where he was engaged in the manufacture of an anti-hog cholera cure, when he entered the army. He was a graduate of the Kansas State Agricultural college.

IN HONOR OF HERO

Flag at Half Mast in Fredonia—Services Today.

Fredonia, July 2.—(Special)—With the flag standing at half mast in the public square, the remains of Lieut. Harry F. Hunt arrived here from overseas today. The lieutenant's command was in the 130th field artillery, 35th division. He died from the effects of gas at Sampigny, France, February 6, 1918. Open-air services in courthouse park will be held at 10 o'clock Sunday, conducted by former Chaplain J. Ashton Davies.

BURY LIEUTENANT HUNT

Body Arrived Here from France, Saturday Morning—Funeral Sunday.

Fredonia's flag floated at half mast, Saturday and Sunday in honor of Lieutenant Harry Hunt, who died in France. The body arrived here from Hoboken, New Jersey, Saturday morning, and funeral services were held Sunday morning at ten o'clock, from the courthouse lawn. The services were in charge of the Charles Walters Post, American Legion, Rev. J. A. Davies, making the address. Lieut. Hunt was accorded a military burial, Legion members in uniform acting as an escort of honor and as pall bearers. The last salute was fired over the grave.

Harry Hunt was the son of Frank Hunt and Annie Brindle, and was born in Fredonia. Mr. Hunt was at that time superintendent of the water works. Later the family moved to Colorado, but Mr. Hunt was killed in an accident in a Colorado mine, and Mrs. Hunt returned to Wilson-co. with her two children, Frank and Nellie, and lived on the John Brindle farm for a number of years. Here the children finished common school at the Grand Valley schoolhouse.

Desiring higher education for her family, Mrs. Hunt moved to Manhattan, where Frank graduated from the State Agricultural college. He completed the veterinary course, and was with a serum company in Wichita, when war was declared. He served overseas with Veterinary Unit, 130 F. A., as second lieutenant until his death which was caused by monoxide gas.

Mrs. Hunt is living at Manhattan at present. Lieutenant Hunt was a nephew of George Brindle, of Fredonia, John Brindle, of Lafontaine, and Misses Nell and Flora Brindle.

From "Veterinary Military History of the United States," Vol. II, by Merillat and Campbell, pages 982 and 1045:

The Veterinary Officers of the World War

*2nd Lieut. HARRY FRANK HUNT, Kansas. Com. 2nd lieut. July 20, 1917; died Feb. 6, 1919; duty, 87th Div.,Camp Pike, Ark., Sept., 1917; 312th Amm. Train; A.E.F., March, 1918; died at Champigny, France, from carbon monoxide gas.

(Names marked with an asterisk (*) indicate that the officer died while in the military service.)

STATE OF KANSAS
THE ADJUTANT GENERAL'S OFFICE

Certificate of Service

THIS IS TO CERTIFY, That the records of this office show Military Service of

HARRY   F.   HUNT .... as follows:
Officer -- ORC White**

Residence: Wichita, Kansas

Born in Fredonia, Kansas on November 9, 1890

Called into active service as 2nd. Lt. Vet. Corps Sept. 18/17 fr.ORC

Promotions :----------

Organizations and
   staff assignments: 312 Am.Tr. 87 Div. to Sept. 28/18; 110 Tn.Hq. & M. P.
                      35th Div. to Jan. 9/19; Vet. Unit 10 69th Inf. Brig.
                      to 130 F. A. to death.

Principal stations: Camp Pike Ark; AEF;

Engagements: ---------------

Wounds received in action: None

Served overseas: March 14/1918 to death

Died: February 6,1919 Monoxide-Gas; Sampigny,France

Buried at: -------------

Person notified of death: Mrs. Annie S. Hunt(Mother)

Address: 1010 Bluemont ave., Manhattan, Kansas

IN TESTIMONY WHEREOF, I have hereunto set my hand and affixed my official seal, at

the capitol, in the city of Topeka, this....**3rd**....day of......December................192..4

R. Niele Rahn
....
The Adjutant General of Kansas.

9-4115

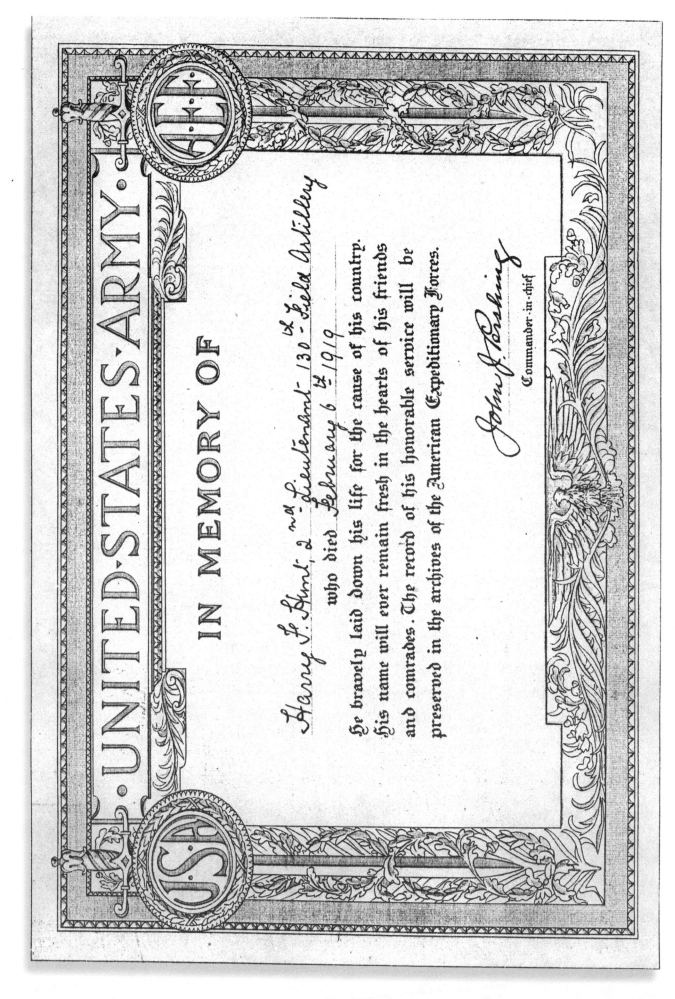

UNITED·STATES·ARMY·

IN MEMORY OF

Harry F. Hunt, 2nd Lieutenant, 130th Field Artillery

who died February 6th 1919

He bravely laid down his life for the cause of his country. His name will ever remain fresh in the hearts of his friends and comrades. The record of his honorable service will be preserved in the archives of the American Expeditionary Forces.

John J. Pershing

Commander-in-chief

Kansas State Agricultural College

Lt. Merle W. Converse,
who married Nellie

Annie reads her son's letters

Lt. and Mrs. Merle W. Converse
February 20th, 1919

Nellie in 1919

FUNERAL NOTICE

Died, at Sampigny, France, on February 6th, 1919

Lieut. HARRY F. HUNT

130th Field Artillery, 35th Division, A. E. F.
Funeral services will be held from the court house
lawn on Sunday, July 3d, 1921, at 10 o'clock, a. m.
The Rev. J. Ashton Davies, officiating.
Interment in the Fredonia cemetery.
Charles Walters Post, American Legion, in charge.

Harry - 1919

Annie

Ralph and Leland Brindle
attended Lt. Hunt's burial in 1921

Leland, Ralph and Jayne Brindle

Nellie with her chicks, and Annie

Nellie b. 1895

Harry b. 1920

Verne b. 1921

Betty b. 1923

Virginia b. 1925

Faye b. 1927

Ruth b. 1930

Ramona b. 1932

Merle Edward b. 1936, Annie b. 1866, Harriet Jane b. 1937

EPILOGUE

Annie continued to live in her home at 1010 Bluemont Street in Manhattan, and she operated her boarding house for many more years.

Gussie's last name, and her life after Lt. Hunt's death, are not known.

Nellie and Merle were married in Annie's home on February 20, 1919. They lived on a farm in Wabaunsee County, Kansas, then moved to Idaho for a time before returning to Kansas. Eventually they settled on Pine Crest Farm nine miles south of Eskridge.

Nellie and Merle were parents of nine children, six daughters and three sons. They named their first-born, a son, Harry Hunt after Nellie's brother. In birth order, the others are Verne Warren, Betty Anne, Virginia Myrle, Faye Daphne, Ruth Nadine, Ramona Nell, Merle Edward and Harriet Jane. Annie referred to them as "Nellie's chicks" and was a doting grandmother.

Annie's last boarder was her nephew, Ralph Brindle. Through the years other relatives, including the author of this book, lived in the upstairs bedrooms while attending Kansas State Agricultural College, now Kansas State University.

Annie suffered a stroke in 1948. For the last three months of her life, Nellie and this author took care of her, and both were at her bedside when she died in St. Mary's Hospital at age 83. She was laid to rest August 12, 1949, in the Fredonia City Cemetery in Wilson County, Kansas, near the two most-beloved men in her life—her husband, Frank, and her son, Harry.

Nellie and Merle retired in Eskridge. He died of pneumonia in 1961 at age 65. Surrounded by family and friends, Nellie lived for 20 more years. She died of cancer in April, 1981, at age 85. At the first printing of "Letters Home" all of their children survive.

BIBLIOGRAPHY

1. "Final Report of Gen. John J. Pershing, Commander-in-chief, American Expeditionary Forces," Washington Government Printing Office, 1920.

2. "Veterinary Military History of the United States," Volume I, by Louis A. Merillat, Lt. Col., Vet.-Res., Chief Veterinarian, First Army, American Expeditionary Forces, and Delwin M. Campbell, Lt. Col., Vet.-Res., Editor, Veterinary Medicine, Chicago, U.S.A., Veterinary Magazine Corp., 1935.

3. "Veterinary Military History of the United States," Volume II, by Louis A. Merillat, Lt. Col., Vet.-Res., Chief Veterinarian, First Army, American Expeditionary Forces, and Delwin M. Campbell, Lt. Col., Vet.-Res., Editor, Veterinary Medicine, Kansas City, MO., The Haver-Glover Laboratories, 1935.

ABOUT THE AUTHOR

The author is the fifth child of Nellie and Merle Converse, born at home on July 21, 1927, ten years and one day after her uncle, Harry Frank Hunt, received his commission as second lieutenant.

She attended a rural one-room elementary school, District 44, for eight years and was graduated at age 17 from Eskridge Rural High School. As the nation was engaged in World War II, she went to work in the Santa Fe Railroad offices in Topeka until the war ended.

At the urging of her mother, the author majored in journalism and home economics, earning a degree from Kansas State Agricultural College in 1950. She was with "Household" and "Capper's Farmer" magazines in Topeka before her marriage to John L. Brown III. They are parents of two sons, Kevin and Steven.

The family moved to Marysville, Kansas, in 1963. A few years later Faye became a part-time reporter/feature writer for the weekly newspaper, "The Marysville Advocate," published by a pair of Kansas State graduates, Howard and Sharon Kessinger.

A resident of Tucson, Arizona, since 1984, Faye is now a freelance writer. For more than 10 years she has contributed to "Arizona Senior World" newspapers published by Steve and Mary Fish and edited by Gilbert Moore.

She is a member of The Society of Southwestern Authors; Chapter BB PEO; Cary Post No. 28, American Legion Auxiliary, the Huachuca Museum Society, and the Alumni Association of Kansas State University.

When her son, Kevin, started asking about his great-uncle, Lt. Harry Frank Hunt, Faye began to gather information. The result is "Letters Home."